54 CAMPUSES.
28 COUNTRIES.
1 AMAZING CAREER.

DEGREE, DIPLOMA & CERTIFICATE COURSES IN:

ANIMATION | AUDIO | DESIGN | FILM | GAMES | WEB & MOBILE

ENROL NOW SAE.EDU.AU
COURSE ENQUIRIES CALL **1800 SAE EDU**
Brisbane | Byron Bay | Sydney | Melbourne | Adelaide | Perth

CRICOS: 00312F
RTO: 0273

ENTRIES ARE NOW OPEN!

THE ATOM PHOTO COMP 2017

THIS YEAR'S THEME IS 'MY BACKYARD'.

The inaugural ATOM Photo Comp in 2016 was a great success, with over 700 entries received across three categories.

This year, we are expanding the competition to five categories, including an 'Open' category for adults.

Prizes include five Canon EOS 700D cameras (RRP: $1029), generously donated by Ted's Cameras.

TAKE 3 original photographs that adddress this year's theme (go online for more info)

SUBMIT your 3 photos through our online entry system at **atomphotocomp.org**

WRITE a short statement (no more than 300 words) and submit it with your entry.

- All photographs must be taken specifically for the ATOM Photo Comp 2017. All entries must be submitted online at atomphotocomp.org.
- Separate categories for Lower Primary (F–3), Upper Primary (4–6), Lower Secondary (7–9), Upper Secondary (10–12) and Open.

The ATOM Photo Comp 2017 is free to enter and is open to all Australian and New Zealand residents.

ENTER YOUR PHOTOGRAPHS NOW!

atomphotocomp.org

Entries close midday AEST, Friday 1 September 2017

Contents

No. 86 // 2017

YEAR LEVEL GUIDE
- P PRIMARY Foundation – Year 6
- MY MIDDLE YEARS Years 4–9
- SS SENIOR SECONDARY Years 10–12

These categories are only intended as a guide. Please read individual articles to determine their suitability for your classroom.

New & Notable

8. **SLUMBER PARTY** MY SS
   Girl Asleep and Growing into Growing Up
   ANNA KUCH AND BRIDGET HANNA

18. **ISLAND IDOLS** P
    Custom, Courage and Culture in Disney's *Moana*
    CAROLYN LESLIE

28. **TEMPORAL TRUTHS** MY SS
    The Girl Who Leapt Through Time
    SUSAN BYE

Talking Society

34. **'I'M A BADASS HUNKY DUDE'** MY SS
    Gender, Hegemony and *She's the Man*
    ADOLFO ARANJUEZ

Screens in the Classroom

42. **CINEMA SCIENCE** SS
    Passengers and the Specifics of Space
    DAVID CREWE

50. **KIDS ON FILM** MY
    Teaching Documentary in the English Classroom
    LOUISE LAVERY

Filmmaker Profile

56. **RICHARD LINKLATER** SS
    ANTHONY CAREW

Teaching Media

72. **MARVEL AND THE STORYTELLING INDUSTRY** SS
    Characters in an Age of Media Convergence
    TYSON WILS

82. **LIGHT THROUGH THE DARKNESS** SS
    Using CAMELS to Analyse Steve McQueen's *Hunger*
    JEREMY GUZMAN

88. **ACTIVE AUDIENCES** SS
    Lessons on Media Agency and Control
    DEBORAH SPILSBURY

94. **PACKING A PUNCH** P MY SS
    Structuring a Short Comedy Film
    VINCENT PICKERING

Tech'd Out

100. **SYNC OR SWIM** P MY SS
     Adobe Premiere Clip
     KEVIN LAVERY

106. **VIRTUAL TOOLKIT** P MY SS
     JANE SHIELDS

Film as Text

110. **BEST IN THE WEST**
     Genre, John Wayne and the American Dream in John Ford's *The Searchers*
     BRIAN MCFARLANE

116. **'HEY, THAT'S NO DAME!'**
     Comedy and Performance in *Some Like It Hot*
     ELOISE ROSS

122. **LOOKING FOR A WAY OUT**
     Reimagining the Gaze in *Carol*
     GABRIELLE O'BRIEN

Screen EDUCATION
No. 86

WWW.SCREENEDUCATION.COM.AU

Managing Editor
Peter Tapp
editor@atom.org.au

Editor
Greta Parry
screen_ed@atom.org.au

Subeditor
Adolfo Aranjuez

Editorial Committee
Lee Burton (Vic.)
Anne Cloonan (Primary Consultant)
Christine Evely (Vic.)
Michael Dezuanni (Qld)

Art Director
Heidi McKinnon

Subscriptions & Online Services
Zak Hamer

Subscriptions & Online Services Assistants
Will Allen, Anne van der Sanden

Printing
Shenzhen Tian Hong Printing

Advertising
Peter Tapp
+61 (412) 473 116
editor@atom.org.au

facebook.com/screeneducation
twitter.com/screeneducation

ISBN 978-1-76061-085-2
ISSN 1449-857X © ATOM 2017
Published June 2017

If you have an activity that has worked well for you in the classroom, please submit it for publication. We have a style guide for contributors, which is available from our website (below). Submit articles by email as an attachment, in Microsoft Word, and graphics as attachments saved as Photoshop, TIFF or JPEG files.

WEB www.screeneducation.com.au
POST ATOM
PO Box 2040
St Kilda West VIC 3182
Australia
TEL +61 (3) 9525 5302
EMAIL screen_ed@atom.org.au

Chair — Roger Dunscombe
Deputy Chair — Victoria Giummarra
Education Executive Officer — Robert Young
Publications & Awards Manager — Peter Tapp
Committee Members — Lisa Worthy
Kevin Tibaldi
Jenna Grace
Matthew Bon
Emma McCulloch
Jessica Lee
Education Officer — Bec Mackey

Associate Editors for refereed articles

FELICITY COLLINS
Associate Professor,
Department of
Cinema Studies,
La Trobe University

MICHAEL DEZUANNI
Associate Professor,
Film and Media Studies,
Queensland University
of Technology

ANNA DZENIS
Lecturer, Department
of Cinema Studies,
La Trobe University

BERYL EXLEY
Associate Professor,
Faculty of Education,
Queensland University
of Technology

TRISH FITZSIMONS
Associate Professor,
Griffith Film School,
Griffith University

BEN GOLDSMITH
Senior Lecturer, Screen
and Media, University of
the Sunshine Coast

ANITA JETNIKOFF
Senior Lecturer, School
of Cultural and Language
Studies in Education,
Queensland University
of Technology

BRIAN McFARLANE
Adjunct Professor, Institute
for Social Research, Swinburne
University of Technology

JANE MILLS
Associate Professor,
Senior Research Fellow,
Journalism and Media
Research Centre, UNSW

LORRAINE MORTIMER
Honorary Associate,
Department of
Anthropology,
University of Sydney

SUE TURNBULL
Professor,
School of Social Sciences,
Media & Communication,
University of Wollongong

CONSTANTINE VEREVIS
Associate Professor,
Film and Screen Studies,
Monash University

MIKE WALSH
Associate Professor,
Department of
Screen and Media,
Flinders University

DEANE WILLIAMS
Associate Professor,
Film and Screen Studies,
Monash University

BRIAN YECIES
Senior Lecturer,
Communication and
Cultural Studies,
Faculty of Arts,
University of Wollongong

AUDREY YUE
Senior Lecturer,
Department of English
and Cultural Studies,
University of Melbourne

AUSTRALIAN TEACHERS OF MEDIA

Screen Education is indexed by APAIS and the Australian Film Institute's Research and Information department.

Metro has something for everyone

▲ **ISSUE 191**

Girl Asleep. Down Under. Killing Ground. Barracuda. The Kettering Incident. The films of Park Chan-wook. *The Wailing. Spa Night. The Family. Hotel Coolgardie. Tickled. Winter at Westbeth. Alvin Purple.** Screen media opportunities in the education sector.

▲ **ISSUE 190**

Goldstone. Cleverman. Hunt for the Wilderpeople. The films of Lav Diaz. *Barakah Meets Barakah. Ten Years. Chasing Asylum. Destination Arnold. Embrace.* Sex discourse on screen. *The Bachelor* and reality dating. *Born to Dance* and the dance film. *Palm Beach.**

▲ **ISSUE 189**

Spear. Early Winter. Observance. Pawno. The Family Law. Here Come the Habibs. Mustang. Our Little Sister. Dheepan. Among the Believers. Afghanistan: Inside Australia's War. Remembering the Man. Australian cinema's box-office boom in 2015.

▲ **ISSUE 188**

The Daughter. Looking for Grace. Life. Tanna. A Month of Sundays. The Principal. The films of Naomi Kawase. *Journey to the Shore. Cemetery of Splendour. Putuparri and the Rainmakers. Shock Room. The Silences. The Big Steal.** Animation today. Indie games.

Pick up a copy of Australia's oldest and most respected screen magazine.

Whether you're an avid film fan or a seasoned theorist, you will find pieces that pique your interest in *Metro*.

Every issue features long-form reviews, interviews and essays on film, television and media – new and old – from Australia, New Zealand and the Asia-Pacific region.

◄ **ISSUE 192**

Lion. Joe Cinque's Consolation. Boys in the Trees. Spin Out. Deep Water. Rosehaven. The Salesman. After the Storm. Happy Hour. Three. Zach's Ceremony. Collisions. On Richard's Side. Baxter and Me. Meal Tickets and rock'n'roll. *Ella*, Indigeneity and ballet. *The Love Letters from Teralba Road.** The *Shine* campaign. The *Screen Currency* report.

* Part of the NFSA's Kodak/Atlab Cinema Collection

TO PURCHASE: Visit The Education Shop at <http://theeducationshop.com.au>.
Issues are $19.95 plus P&H (inc. GST).

Individual articles from back issues are also available as PDF downloads from The Education Shop.

THE EDUCATION SHOP IS NOW STREAMING VIDEO CONTENT

THE EDUCATION SHOP IS AN ONLINE REPOSITORY FOR TEACHERS, LECTURERS, STUDENTS AND PARENTS AT PRIMARY, SECONDARY AND TERTIARY LEVELS.

ATOM has nearly **50 years** of experience in catering to educators.

OFFERING VIDEO CONTENT IN A STREAMING FORMAT WILL ENSURE THE EDUCATION SHOP MAINTAINS ITS ROLE AS A ONE-STOP SHOP FOR TEACHERS AND STUDENTS.

Covering all curriculum areas, including the arts, humanities and sciences

The Education Shop includes thousands of downloadable articles, study guides, interviews and reviews, as well as books and DVDs to help you with teaching and learning. You can also purchase or renew magazine subscriptions and ATOM memberships.

The Education Shop gladly accepts school purchase order numbers as well as credit card and PayPal payments.

theeducationshop.com.au

YEAR 8
HISTORY CLASSROOM

Depth Study units

Depth Study 1

THE WESTERN AND ISLAMIC WORLD + EUROPE AND THE MEDIEVAL WORLD

» The Ottoman Empire (c.1299-c.1683)
» Renaissance Italy (c.1400-c.1600)
» The Vikings (c.790-c.1066)
» Medieval Europe (c.590-c.1500)

Depth Study 2

THE ASIA-PACIFIC WORLD

» Angkor/Khmer Empire (c.802-c.1431)
» Japan Under the Shoguns (c.794-1867)
» Mongol Expansion (c.1206-c.1368) (Vic)
» The Polynesian Expansion Across the Pacific (c.700-1756)

Depth Study 3

EXPANDING CONTACTS + DISCOVERY AND EXPLORATION

» Mongol Expansion (c.1206-c.1368)
» The Black Death in Asia, Europe and Africa (14th Century Plague)
» The Spanish Conquest of the Americas (c.1492-c.1572)
» Aboriginal and Indigenous Peoples, Colonisation and Contact History (NSW)

Each Depth Study resource is $20 (incl GST) + Postage and handling

To order go to: **theeducationshop.com.au**

SLUMBER PARTY

GIRL ASLEEP AND GROWING INTO GROWING UP

www.screeneducation.com.au

In this uniquely Australian and highly theatrical coming-of-age tale, a teenage girl faces the loss of her childhood with the help of surreal dreamscapes and quirky characters, write ANNA KUCH and BRIDGET HANNA.

Girl Asleep (Rosemary Myers, 2015) tells the story of Greta (Bethany Whitmore) as she struggles through school and home life in the lead-up to her fifteenth birthday. Receiving critical acclaim across the globe, the film offers a spectacularly refreshing alternative for Australian cinema through its exploration of the teenage fantasy narrative with an absurd yet enchanting Aussie twist. *Girl Asleep* is also the perfect Australian coming-of-age story to study with secondary students. The narrative explores, as writer Matthew Whittet comments, 'a young girl's journey into figuring out who she doesn't want to be'.[1]

THEATRICAL PRODUCTION AND AUSTRALIAN TONE

Girl Asleep was originally a stage play, also written by Whittet and directed by Myers. The film contains continuous references to the story's original medium through the manipulation of production elements: close-ups of facial expressions, lingering symmetrical shots and a stylised colour palette that matches the 1970s setting of the film. Many reviewers have likened the aesthetic to those of *Napoleon Dynamite* (Jared Hess, 2004), *Donnie Darko* (Richard Kelly, 2001) and the films of Wes Anderson.[2] As well as drawing on these self-consciously idiosyncratic worlds, the stylised features of *Girl Asleep* also relate to the theatre's exaggeration of facial expressions, gesture and body language, and such theatrical production features as striking make-up and costumes and vibrant set design.

The film, shot in 4:3 aspect ratio, constantly restricts the audience's view in a similar way to the stage: there is a clear line of sight, everything coordinates and the mise en scène is intricately curated. We are steered throughout the entire film to focus on certain elements of cinematography, such as specific shot types and length of takes, which at times draw attention to the costuming and production design.

The theatrical elements of *Girl Asleep* lend the film an offbeat, quirky tone that tempers the melancholic, dark aspects of the story with humour. The stage-like mise en scène of Greta's awkward moments, alone in the playground or confronted by the popular girls, Jade (Maiah Stewardson), Amber (Fiona Dawson) and Sapphire (Grace Dawson), emphasise the painful nature of these

PREVIOUS SPREAD, L-R: Greta (Bethany Whitmore); Greta with Adam / Benoit Tremet (Eamon Farren) during a dream sequence THIS PAGE, FROM TOP: Greta in her bedroom; Greta with her mother, Janet (Amber McMahon, left), and older sister, Genevieve (Imogen Archer)

encounters. However, this staging also infuses these moments with a mocking playfulness. While we feel for Greta as she sits alone on a bench in the middle of the frame, we are distracted and amused by a series of tableau-like dramas enacted behind her.

The exaggerated characterisation of Greta's parents, Conrad (Whittet) and Janet (Amber McMahon), also adds a humorous tone to the film. Conrad is the epitome of the daggy dad, telling bad jokes and talking playfully to Greta as if she were a little girl. His tragicomic character is simultaneously pathetic, amusing and cringeworthy, especially when placed in contrast with Adam (Eamon Farren), a 'ladies man'. Janet is another figure who is a combination of tragic and comic. Her fierce arguments with Conrad and Genevieve (Imogen Archer), Greta's older sister, and her appearance in Greta's dream as the Frozen Woman, point to unhappiness, despite the comedy inherent in her themed outfit for the family meal, her theatrical responses to Adam's flirting and the way she asserts her parental authority while pedalling on an exercise bike.

- How are different shot types and lighting used to set the mood in different scenes?
- Why do the filmmakers choose to make Greta's parents both tragic and comic? How does it add to their characterisation? What does it say about Greta's relationship with her parents?
- In her 1964 essay 'Notes on "Camp"', Susan Sontag wrote, 'the essence of Camp is its love of the unnatural: of artifice and exaggeration'.[3] To what extent does *Girl Asleep* fit this definition?

ABOVE: Greta with school friend Elliott (Harrison Feldman), who develops romantic feelings for her

FRIENDSHIP, IDENTITY AND SEXUALITY

Girl Asleep explores notions of friendship, sexuality and identity in the Australian teen experience. Greta and Elliott's (Harrison Feldman) relationship is an interesting exploration of the often difficult terrain of friendship between a heterosexual teen girl and boy. Elliott is a self-described easygoing person. He tells Greta, 'I'm happy to just go with the flow, actually. I find it's the best way to be friendly with people,' and yet it is difficult for Greta to be easygoing in her friendship with Elliott, especially after he declares that he is attracted to her. Greta is uncharacteristically cruel in her rejection of Elliott's advances, showing her uncertainty about what kind of relationship she wants with him and how she wants to identify herself sexually. Perhaps Elliott's desire suggests to Greta an identity similar to 'crazy eyes' Denise (Danielle Catanzariti), a girl who is attracted to Elliott and is portrayed as ridiculous with her panting eagerness and grotesque make-up and attire. Alternatively, perhaps she doesn't find Elliott attractive sexually and is disturbed by what this might mean for her identity as a girl transitioning into womanhood. She demands that Elliott label her as 'frigid', a sexual identity that sits in opposition to those performed by both Denise and the popular girls. However, when the popular girls publicly label Greta as 'frigid', she is horrified and flees to her bedroom and her dream world.

Positioned between childhood and adulthood, Greta finds herself alternately lured towards and repelled by the male characters in the film and the sexuality they represent. She rejects taking on an active sexual identity like her sister and the popular girls at school, but experiments with being sexually passive. When confronted with Adam's flirtatious behaviour, her attention is drawn to him but she remains frozen in place, unable or unwilling to respond to him in the way that either her mother or sister might. However, in Greta's dream, the singer Benoit Tremet (also

> Positioned between childhood and adulthood, Greta finds herself alternately lured towards and repelled by the male characters in the film and the sexuality they represent.

played by Farren) acts for her. He seems to hypnotise her, telling her exactly what she wants and what he will do to her, and despite her protests, pushes her onto the bed and tells her he's 'going to make her a woman'. The uncomfortable and sinister tone of this scene could represent Greta's unconscious recognition of the potential loss of agency, or even danger, inherent in exploring sex with someone like Adam.

While Greta's friendship with Elliott is fraught by complications after he declares his desire for her, female friendship with other teen girls is also presented as an unappealing option for her. Her Finnish penpal is on the other side of the world, and the friendship offered by girls from her own class demands conformity and is filled with menace. The only way to be accepted into their group is to comply with their way of being – there is no space for Greta's individual voice, and no freedom to decide whether she 'feels like it or not'. These girls represent a way of being that doesn't interest Greta, and because she won't adopt their version of female sexuality, their venom targets her in precisely those terms. They declare she is 'frigid', has 'no tits' and wears clothes that make her 'look like a twelve-year-old boy'. This relationship between Greta and the popular girls conforms to a common trope in popular culture whereby female friendship is portrayed as malicious, poisonous or competitive.

Genevieve offers neither companionship nor a model of identity that Greta is keen to take on herself. However, she does offer Greta reassurance that this difficult and troubling transitional experience won't last. Genevieve represents the possibility of becoming a woman who is confident in her sexual identity and happy to actively pursue her desires. When she tells Greta, 'You're not alone,' she is not offering her sister friendship, but rather informing her that other women have experienced this difficult time and survived it, finding their identity on the other side.

- Can you think of other films that portray female friendship as malicious, poisonous or competitive? Why might this be a trope in films?
- Does the film end with Greta discovering her own sexual identity? What evidence from the film supports your answer?

DREAMS, TRANSITIONS AND FAIRYTALES

The dream sequence begins after Jade and her lackeys humiliate Greta, and Elliott confesses his desire to be more than friends. The difference between the dream world and reality is blurred; the characters metamorphose into extreme versions of themselves, whereby a single aspect of their personality is amplified

Everyday teenage concerns become immediate physical dangers in Greta's subconscious.

The reference to the title, 'Girl Asleep', plays out literally on screen as the dream acts as a transitional rehearsal stage – a liminal space for Greta to respond to her parents' opposing views, and to explore whether to become a woman or to remain a girl. The dream is prompted by Greta's music box, which causes her to fall on her bed asleep. She 'wakes' in her room to see a figure in a yellow robe standing in her doorway holding the music box. Throughout this sequence, the music box acts as a connection to Greta's early youth. The journey to find it reflects her desires

Fairytales are marked by notions of transition – often, they present the moment when an adolescent female comes of age and must face mythical dangers in order to move forward to her happily ever after. In *Girl Asleep*, danger seems to lurk in multiple places: high-school bathrooms, home, and the overshadowing forest beyond the backyard fence.

in a way that references the fantastical world of *The Wizard of Oz* (Victor Fleming, 1939). As in many fairytales, Greta's dream reflects her concerns in the real world. Fairytales are marked by notions of transition – often, they present the moment when an adolescent female comes of age and must face mythical dangers in order to move forward to her happily ever after. In *Girl Asleep*, danger seems to lurk in multiple places: high-school bathrooms, home, and the overshadowing forest beyond the backyard fence.

to hold onto her childhood and avoid the questions that come with adulthood, especially those just posed by Elliott. The robed figure encourages Greta to follow it into the backyard, over the fence and into the forest beyond, reminding us of Alice's surreal journey down the rabbit hole.

As Greta enters the forest, the vibrant and multifaceted colour palette used in the party scenes is replaced by monochrome dark greys and shadows; it is only when Greta reaches a clearing that

THIS PAGE, FROM TOP: Greta in her dream world; the popular girls from Greta's school (Maiah Stewardson, and Fiona and Grace Dawson); The Huldra (Tilda Cobham-Hervey)

colour re-emerges in her clothing. The magic of the woods traps her within the clearing as long tree stumps appear from nowhere and enclose her. Like Greta, we know there is no going back. Time and space know no bounds here. The forest's occupants could be said to portray the other teenagers from the party, like Greta, in transition to adulthood. The manipulation of editing techniques allow the forest characters to glide around as if they are being put in fast forward, and jump cuts allow them to appear out of thin air and replace other characters at a moment's notice. This heightened absurdity highlights the film medium and draws attention to the magic of Greta's dreamscape.

As the yellow-robed figure retreats into the woods, Greta goes on a journey to find it, meeting various characters along the way. The first is The Huldra (Tilda Cobham-Hervey), the Scandinavian forest creature from her Finnish penpal's letter. The Huldra offers Greta a model of powerful womanhood that she can aspire to, and which is missing from her life. However, The Huldra draws on Greta's uncertainty, questioning her maturity and suggesting she is 'not ready for this place' and is 'just a little girl'.

The sound of barking dogs introduces a farcical element to the dream sequence as Greta and The Huldra run from the perceived danger. In fact, they are clearly just running on the spot, as the forest moves past them. After The Huldra calls her horse, the action continues, becoming increasingly ludicrous. The horse's head is deliberately fake, alluding to the film's theatrical origins, but the audience's expectations are overturned when a live horse enters the frame, a joke that also has the effect of connecting us with Greta's coming of age. The horse is a representation of Greta's journey towards adult sexuality, as the toy horses that adorn her bedroom shelves become a fabricated horse that then becomes a live stallion.

- If the forest is a space of transition into adulthood, what is the significance of the forest characters who are adults?

- Can you think of other coming-of-age narratives that use similar dream sequences?
- Research the Scandinavian folklore of The Huldra. Drawing on this knowledge, what do you think The Huldra represents in the dream sequence?

During the dream sequence, Greta comes across her father and mother in the forms of the Abject Man and the Frozen Woman. According to Dino Felluga, Julia Kristeva's definition of the abject is the 'human reaction to a threatened breakdown in meaning caused by the loss of the distinction between subject and object or between self and other'.[4] The inherent danger in abject things or people repels but also fascinates at the same time. Conrad as the Abject Man encompasses this idea for Greta. She is drawn to and disgusted by her father; he is what she wants in a parent but not in a potential partner. This is represented in the dream sequence by his appearance as a decaying zombie, but also in the real world when he is dressed in uncomfortably tiny shorts and overbearingly tucking Greta into bed. The Abject Man is holding onto Greta's childhood through the music box. It is his way of keeping her close, protecting her and remaining relevant as a father. He is in denial about his daughter growing up, and as much as Greta wants to laugh at his 'dad jokes' to keep him happy, she is also nauseated by his neediness and wants her freedom.

Greta comes across the Frozen Woman in a cave of music boxes. Dressed in white, she resembles a fairytale ice queen. Greta asks the Frozen Woman if she has seen the music box, which prompts the woman to aggressively destroy the music box she has in her arms. She breaks the music boxes 'because they were not the right one. They were not the beautiful song. The one I remember from my youth full of promise and love.' In Greta's dream, her mother represents lost hope, which contributes to Greta's fear of

growing up. We can also connect this figure to that of the 1970s Stepford housewife who is outwardly positive, productive and obedient but is actually dissatisfied with her life. The possibility that Greta's mother may not be happy with her adult life feeds into Greta's fear of growing up and what awaits her in the future. The atmosphere of this scene is rigid and cold to reflect the sorrow felt by the Frozen Woman. The viewer's attention is drawn towards the movement in the scene, which seems delayed and stunted, heightening the characters' inability to move forward or backward, stuck in regret in this liminal space.

- Explore Kristeva's notion of the abject. Apart from the Abject Man, what else does Greta find repellent and attractive at the same time?
- Why is the Frozen Woman looking wistfully into her past in this scene? What do we learn about Greta's mother in the real world that might suggest she is unhappy with her life?
- What does the Frozen Woman mean when she says, 'You and I, we're the same. You're just like me now,' and why does it scare Greta?

CONFRONTING GROWING PAINS

During the final act of the dream, Greta goes on a rampage, ransacking her own bedroom, destroying everything that reminds her of her childhood. The yellow-robed character appears in the doorway. Still angry, Greta walks up to the creature and takes the music box out of its hands, reclaiming her childhood. The base of the robe moves and a child crawls out from underneath. We realise it is our protagonist as a child (Lucy Cowan). Greta asks, 'All this was you?' to which the child Greta answers, 'No, silly, it was you.' The child picks up one of the horse figurines and teenage Greta tucks in and lies down with young Greta. It's a fitting goodbye to her childhood and a show of acceptance that things

> Importantly, Greta realises she does not need to let go of the person she was as she moves forward.

are changing. Importantly, however, Greta realises she does not need to let go of the person she was as she moves forward. They fall asleep together and the next minute, Greta wakes up in her room, with the party raging on downstairs. This moment in the dream sequence portrays Greta's transition: she has just stood up to her demons and destroyed her childhood room, and now feels a sense of loss, longing and melancholia.

- Throughout the dream, creatures of the forest offer Greta paper cranes with notes. One of these reads, 'Find the girl with the tiny hands'. These act as tips or tricks for surviving the forest, and allude to the 'eat me' and 'drink me' notes from *Alice in Wonderland*. What does the note mean? If the girl with the tiny hands is Greta as a child, is it asking Greta to find herself?
- Why do you think the child Greta wanted older Greta to follow her into the forest? Was child Greta encouraging older Greta to move forward in her transition to adulthood?
- How does the dream sequence reflect the idea that *Girl Asleep* is a film about finding out who you *don't* want to be?

Adam with Greta's father, Conrad (Matthew Whittet)

The conclusion of the film encompasses the idea that in order to find out who you are, you might need to first explore things that don't appeal to you. Throughout the film, Greta is pressured to adopt various identities by her family, her friend Elliott and her other peers, and we see the distress and confusion that this causes her. Towards the end of the film, we see a car rocking up and down in Greta's driveway and the audience's expectations are turned on their heads as Greta and Elliott emerge from the car having changed outfits. They rejoin the party, Greta now in Elliott's blue suit and Elliott in Greta's pink dress. This final scene shows Greta comfortable and happy doing what she wants, as herself, and really owning that decision.

https://clickv.ie/w/screen-ed/girl-asleep

Bridget Hanna and Anna Kuch are education deliverers at the Australian Centre for the Moving Image. **SE**

Endnotes

[1] Matthew Whittet, quoted in Elizabeth Flux, 'Dream Sequence: Rosemary Myers' *Girl Asleep* and Cinematic Coming of Age', *Metro*, no. 191, Summer 2017, p. 8.
[2] See Eddie Cockrell, 'Film Review: *Girl Asleep*', *Variety*, 15 February 2016, <http://variety.com/2016/film/festivals/girl-asleep-review-berlin-film-festival-1201706358/>; Karl Quinn, 'How *Girl Asleep*, Australia's Answer to *Napoleon Dynamite*, Made It to the Big Screen', *The Sydney Morning Herald*, 8 September 2016, <http://www.smh.com.au/entertainment/movies/how-girl-asleep-australias-answer-to-napoleon-dynamite-made-it-to-the-big-screen-20160907-gras68.html>; Luke Buckmaster, '*Girl Asleep* Review – as Singular, Enchanting and Expansive as a Young Person's Mind', *The Guardian*, 9 September 2016, <https://www.theguardian.com/film/2016/sep/09/girl-asleep-review-rosemary-myers-bethany-whitmore-harrison-feldman>; and Philippa Hawker, '*Girl Asleep*: Rosemary Myers on Adolescent Dreams, Dagginess, Desires', *The Australian*, 20 August 2016, <http://www.theaustralian.com.au/arts/review/girl-asleep-rosemary-myers-on-adolescent-dreams-dagginess-desires/news-story/3a42c3c768aa1640136043573ed03efe>, all accessed 13 April 2017.
[3] Susan Sontag, 'Notes on "Camp"', in Fabio Cleto (ed.), *Camp: Queer Aesthetics and the Performing Subject, A Reader*, University of Michigan Press, Ann Arbor, 1999, p. 53.
[4] Dino Felluga, 'Modules on Kristeva: On the Abject', *Introductory Guide to Critical Theory*, 2011, <http://www.purdue.edu/guidetotheory/psychoanalysis/kristevaabject.html>, accessed 1 April 2017.

Island Idols

CUSTOM, COURAGE AND CULTURE IN DISNEY'S *MOANA*

CAROLYN LESLIE explores the groundbreaking Disney animation that not only offers an active, relatable heroine, but also engages with the rich cultures of the Pacific Islands.

The latest Disney heroine to grace our screens is a Polynesian self-declared non-princess who will leave the safety of her island in order to save it. She will team up with a demigod and battle fearsome monsters and gods. Along the way she will sing, dance and reconnect her people to their cultural traditions as ocean explorers.

The story of *Moana* takes place around 2000 years ago. Although it is set in the Pacific Islands, the island of Motunui is deliberately fictional. Veteran Disney directors Ron Clements and John Musker, whose films include classics like *The Little Mermaid* (1989) and *The Princess and the Frog* (2009), came up with an idea to make a Pacific Islands–themed movie. They created a team, which became known as the Oceanic Story Trust, with the purpose of ensuring that the storytelling in the movie was respectful and reflective of Polynesian culture. The trust included indigenous elders, artists, musicians and academics.

The role of the trust was not just to advise Clements, Musker and Disney – the trust apparently vetted every detail in the movie-making process, including the names of all the characters, every draft of the script, every change to the script (no matter how small) and the details of the art direction. However, while the trust guided the mainstream non-Polynesian filmmakers (with Disney being *the* archetypal mainstream animation studio), it is inescapable that this is still a tale of, and about, the Pacific Islands mostly told by outsiders. In this way, *Moana*, as a cultural object, opens up questions about who is telling these traditional stories and whether or not it is appropriate for the filmmakers to be doing so.

IN THE TIME OF LONG AGO …

Moana starts with a woman's voice narrating an origin story about the Pacific Islands. We are listening to Gramma Tala (Rachel House) telling us about the time when the mother island, Te Fiti, was green and fertile and creative. Te Fiti is both a mythic being (in that she was a goddess-like creature) and a physical formation (in that 'she' was an island). She possessed a unique form of creativity: Te Fiti could create islands with luscious green ecosystems. Her power emanated from her heart, which took the physical form of a green gem set in the mandala carved into her chest.

But other beings coveted Te Fiti's power. They tried to steal her heart gem. And, one day, someone succeeded. Maui (Dwayne

Johnson), the demigod of wind and sea, used the magical powers of his fishhook to shapeshift and stole Te Fiti's heart gem. He wanted to give it to humans, so that they could create islands of their own, but the result was catastrophic: instead of Te Fiti being a verdant and creative life force, her creations started to rot and crumble away. A great darkness was born.

As Maui tried to escape, the lava god Te Kā arrived and tried to steal the gem from him. A terrible battle between these gods ensued. It ended with both Maui's fishhook and Te Fiti's heart gem lost in the depths of the ocean.

- *Moana*, and the character of Maui in particular, draws on a number of Polynesian origin stories. We hear, in the lyrics of 'You're Welcome', about how Maui created the sun, the sky and the tides. Gramma Tala's stories tell of a time when a goddess transformed herself into a (physical) island. Research an origin story from the Pacific Islands, and find a creative way to tell the story to a contemporary audience.
- Many cultures and societies have origin stories. These may be handed down to us from our elders, or come in the form of religious beliefs. Many contemporary mythological universes also have their own origin stories (such as the Marvel Universe or the *Star Wars* saga). Can you retell one of the origin stories from your culture?
- Create an origin story of your own. You might like to think of a story that explains why something always happens at the same time each year, or how a tradition in your family got started. Or perhaps you would like to create an origin story for a new, made-up society.

MOTUNUI'S CHIEF-IN-TRAINING

The scene pulls back from the origin-story images, and we see that Gramma Tala has been teaching it to a group of Islander toddlers gathered in a school hut. They are living on the island of Motunui, in the middle of the Pacific Ocean. We hear that the darkness unleashed by Maui's theft will one day destroy all the islands. But there is another story, of a time yet to come. In this tale, someone will travel beyond the island reef. That person will find Maui, and restore the heart of Te Fiti. The darkness will be pushed back, and all of the islands will become verdant again.

One tiny girl is excited by these tales more than all the other children. This is Moana (the toddler Moana is voiced by Louise Bush; the teenage Moana, by Auli'i Cravalho). She is the chief's daughter and Gramma Tala's granddaughter. Suddenly, her father, Chief Tui (Temuera Morrison), interrupts the storytelling. He tells another version of events, one that can he can back up with evidence. According to Chief Tui, Motunui is a safe and wonderful place to live. The darkness will not come to their shores. He argues that the people of the village have everything they need right there on the island, and if everyone plays their role in society, then no-one will be at risk. No-one needs to go beyond the reef.

But as Moana grows up, she is constantly drawn to the ocean. (Even her name – Moana – means 'ocean'.) For many Pacific Islands cultures, the ocean is a living, sentient being. In this film, the ocean is seen as a character in its own right, complete with an anthropomorphic physicality. The ocean shows that it is a conscious being through the way it changes its movement (such as when it parts its waves and encourages the toddler Moana to wander out onto a dry ocean bed) and its shape (such as when Moana is sailing her boat and the water swells into a vaguely humanoid shape that can high-five with her). Moana reacts to the ocean as she does with any other character – it is as real to her as Pua, her pet pig, and Heihei (Alan Tudyk), her pet chicken. The ocean beckons to her, it plays with her. At one point, the ocean tries to give her a green gem. But Chief Tui keeps pulling Moana away from the water (and, in one case, away from the gem) and back to the village. There, Moana learns the songs, dances and traditions of her people – the people she will be expected to lead someday.

One day, Chief Tui takes his daughter to a sacred place at the top of a steep hill. Here is a pile of rocks. Every chief in turn has placed a rock on this pile – and one day Moana will place her item on top.

- Does your culture or society expect you to play a particular role?
- Can you give an example of a traditional song, dance or activity that teaches you what your role might be?
- Do you think it is possible for a person to follow a different path in life than the one set out for them?

SUSTAINABLE ENVIRONMENTS

The people of Motunui live in harmony with their natural surroundings. 'Consider the coconut', they sing, celebrating the fruit that supplies food and liquid for their nutritional needs.

It also provides the Islanders with fibre from the shell, which can be used to make netting and other useful tools. The coconut tree supplies shelter from the weather, and its palms can be used as a building material. Chief Tui strongly believes that the island supplies them with all they need to live a rich and fulfilling lifestyle.

But there are signs that this form of living on the land might be in trouble. The villagers are catching fewer fish than they used to. And the coconuts on the island are starting to roll, in a way that echoes the movement of the coconuts in Gramma Tala's stories. Later in the film, Moana has visions of her island becoming rotten and black, with her people hungry and struggling.

- In *Moana*, the environmental threat is seen in mythological terms – destruction of the islands is a result of battles between gods and demigods. But the real Pacific Islands are facing environmental problems due to climate change. Research an area in the Pacific that is being affected by an environmental threat, and find out what the effects on that area are likely to be.
- Chief Tui believes that the island will always offer his people a sustainable way of life, because it always has in the past. What do you think it will take to change his mind?

WHAT'S BEYOND THE REEF?

Even though Moana is drawn to the ocean, and longs to find out about the world beyond the reef, her father is firm. The island is their home, and that reef is their safety barrier – no-one goes sailing beyond it. But her father has his own reasons for not wanting his daughter to venture out into open waters. As Moana's mother, Sina (Nicole Scherzinger), tells her in secret, when Tui was a young man and not yet a chief, he also felt the call of the ocean. Along with his best friend, he attempted to sail beyond the reef. But his one and only attempt to sail into open ocean led to tragedy. His best friend drowned, and Tui nearly did too.

Moana also almost comes to grief in her secretive first attempt to sail into open waters. The ocean is rough and she nearly drowns, before being swept back onto her home beach.

- Like many parents, Chief Tui wants to protect Moana from danger. Do you think his actions are justified?
- Why do you think Moana tries to sail beyond the reef, even though she knows her father almost died doing the same thing?

A HIDDEN HERITAGE

When Moana is washed back onto the shores of Motunui, Gramma Tala finds her and tells her a secret story. It is so secret that Moana must hear it only inside a hidden cave. In the cave, we see depictions of Islanders sailing very large boats, much larger than the small fishing boats that the people of Motunui use inside the reef. There is also a large drum. Gramma Tala instructs Moana to bang the drum to find out who she is meant to be.

After banging the drum, Moana has a vision of people who look like those who live on Motunui, but who are roaming the ocean, using stars as a navigation tool. She hears them sing: 'We are explorers […] We tell the stories of our elders / In a never-ending chain.'

Then Gramma Tala tells another tale of long ago. Their people stopped exploring the seas at the same time that Maui stole Te Fiti's heart gem, because the ocean became full of monsters like Te Kā. They found a safe island and decided to stay there. But Gramma Tala knows that the ocean had tried to give Moana a gem – she was also on the beach that day. Sina joins them, and the two women help Moana prepare to tackle another ocean journey.

Gramma Tala knows she is dying. She knows that saying 'goodbye' to Moana will be her final farewell. She gives Moana a shell-and-twine necklace that has a gem inside it – a green heart gem. It is the gem that Gramma Tala retrieved from the ocean the day that it was given to Moana (and fell from her toddler grasp). Gramma Tala's dying wish is that Moana adventure beyond the reef and find out who she is and who her people can become.

- Why do you think Gramma Tala and Sina help Moana prepare for her ocean voyage, when they know it will be a dangerous undertaking?
- Why do you think Gramma Tala waited until this moment to give Moana the heart gem?

ENCOUNTERS WITH A CELEBRITY DEMIGOD

Moana and Heihei the chicken set sail. The spirit of Gramma Tala (in the form of a stingray) follows them. As they sail beyond the reef, a storm erupts. Moana's sailing skills are not strong enough to handle these conditions. She loses control of her boat and is flipped overboard and into the ocean. Moana passes out, but some time later she and Heihei wake up to find themselves washed ashore on an island, with their boat not far away.

This is the home of Maui, the all-singing demigod with dancing tattoos. Maui has been marooned alone on his island since the battle with Te Kā, because while Maui can do many things, he doesn't have a boat and he can't float (or, apparently, swim).

Maui has a fairly healthy self-esteem, as his song 'You're Welcome!' demonstrates. He has created and/or delivered many good things to humans, including 'the tides, the sun, the sky'. He was only trying to do something nice for humans when he stole Te Fiti's heart gem – not his fault that things went wrong! However, he doesn't get to tell the stories all his own way. His tattoos, which turn up on his skin as he 'earns' them, act like a conscience, moving around his body to show what really happened.

With a boat, Maui can finally leave this island and retrieve his fishhook from the Realm of Monsters, which will restore his shapeshifting powers. He traps Moana in a cave and tries to sail away from the island. But Moana escapes, and together with Heihei, and the help of an ocean wave, gets back on board. She recognises an opportunity – Maui can sail in the open ocean, but has no boat. She has a boat, but doesn't know how to sail it properly. What if he were to teach her to sail, and she could help him retrieve his hook? And then they could return Te Fiti's heart gem …

- Maui's song lists a number of reasons why humans should be grateful to him. Is he correct – should people thank him for what he has done?
- Should Moana believe what Maui says, or what his tattoos show her?
- Maui believes in his own positive publicity. Imagine that Maui was around today. What sort of technology might he use to spread the message about his activities?

A BLINGED-UP CRAB AND AN APPRENTICE WAVE-FINDER

Moana and Maui then travel to the Realm of Monsters to recover Maui's fishhook, which has been lodged in the blinged-up shell of the coconut crab Tamatoa (Jemaine Clement) since the battle with Te Kā. Tamatoa has amassed a cave full of shiny treasure, and is not willing to give up the fishhook, so Moana creates a diversion that allows Maui to get close enough to retrieve the hook.

Now that Maui has his hook back, Moana asks him for a favour. She wants to learn to sail and navigate her boat properly. In Polynesian culture, this is known as being a 'wave-finder'. As she learns her craft, Moana also has some questions about Maui's tattoos. Based on the inked stories, Maui believed he was thrown into the sea as a child because he was not loved by his parents. Wanting to get that love from somewhere, he performed many actions for humans – such as pulling islands out of the ocean with his fishhook. That was the reason he stole Te Fiti's heart gem: he wanted to give it to the humans and bask in their love.

- Being a wave-finder is usually a role reserved for young men. What is the effect of Moana – a young woman – being taught to be a wave-finder?
- Maui has interpreted the stories shown in his tattoos to mean that he was 'unloved' by his parents. Is another interpretation possible?

A LAVA MONSTER AND A DISPIRITED GIRL

If Moana and Maui are going to return the heart gem to Te Fiti, they have to get past Te Kā. Just as they round the straits, Te Kā attacks. Maui battles Te Kā, using his fishhook as both a weapon and a device that allows him to shapeshift. The battle between these gods is ferocious, and Maui's hook is damaged. The damage is severe – if the hook takes one more blow, it will break. 'Without my hook, I'm nothing,' says Maui. To preserve his hook (and his powers), Maui, in the shape of an eagle, flies away from the fight. Moana, meanwhile, is still sailing the boat towards Te Fiti.

Being left on the boat with only Heihei for company, however, rattles Moana. She wants to abandon this quest. She takes the heart gem and throws it back into the ocean. Just then, the spirits of her ancestors visit her – first, her grandmother, and then boats of her travelling ancestors join her on the water. The visit reinvigorates her. She dives into the ocean, retrieves the heart gem, mends her boat and prepares to sail into a battle with Te Kā.

- Do you think that Maui is 'nothing' without his hook? What evidence from the film can you offer to support your argument?

- Why do you think Moana regained her courage when the spirit of her ancestors joined her?
- Have you ever had an experience where you found courage by drawing inspiration from your ancestors?
- Does changing your appearance help you to step up to a battle (or a competition, like playing sport or participating in a school challenge)? What do you do when you put on your 'warrior face'?

REUNITED, AND STRONGER THAN EVER

As she prepares for battle, Moana changes her appearance. She pulls her normally free-flowing hair back into a bun. She puts on her 'warrior face'. She looks for a safe passage through the rocks that will let her land on Te Fiti. And as Te Kā emerges to take her on, Maui reappears. 'I've got your back, chosen one,' he says. He uses his hook one more time to defend Moana – and it is destroyed. Moana is on the island, and she can see the mandala where the heart gem belongs: the spiral is in the middle of Te Kā's chest. Moana puts the heart gem back – and something marvellous starts to happen. The heart gem starts to break up the lava. The angry god Te Kā transforms into the green and fertile goddess Te Fiti. The goddess then starts to rejuvenate the destruction caused by Te Kā: as she touches the lands around her, green leaves start to emerge, and they quickly start to reinvigorate the blackened, dying islands. Where darkness was once spreading across the Pacific, now there are tropical plants and flowers.

- At what point in the film did you understand that Te Kā was an angry version of Te Fiti? What elements in the film indicate that they are different emotional versions of the same being?

'WE KNOW THE WAY'

Te Fiti supplies Moana with a new boat, and Maui with a new hook – after he apologises to her for stealing her heart gem. A new fishhook is not the only new thing in Maui's life – he is now sporting a new tattoo, one that shows his adventures with Moana.

Te Fiti then settles down and transforms into her verdant island form. She is once again a luscious, life-sustaining Pacific island. The regeneration reaches out across the Pacific – as Moana and Maui sail towards her home, we see the formerly dark and crumbling islands (including Motunui) progressively regenerating. The vegetation turns from black to green in front of their eyes. As Motunui rediscovers a luscious version of itself, its inhabitants also rediscover something from their past: the desire to explore what lies beyond the ocean reef is reignited in them. As the Islanders celebrate Moana's return, and the re-greening of their island, they drag the large boats out of the secret cave.

Moana makes a pilgrimage to the sacred place of chiefs. She places a shell, instead of a rock, on top of the traditional pile. Finally, we see the Islanders sailing the large boats out beyond the reef. Moana is steering the boat, while Maui, in eagle form, is flying around the sails. Te Fiti's heart gem has been restored. The oceans are safe again. The islands are healing. Maui's powers are restored. And the people of Motunui have embraced their ancestors' natural penchant for exploration.

Aue, aue
We keep our island in our mind
And when it's time to find home
We know the way.

- Using evidence from the film to support your answer, what do you think happens to Moana and her people in the future? What do you think happens to Maui?
- Moana is going to be chief one day. How do you think her leadership will differ from that of her father, Chief Tui? What effect will this have on the people of Motunui?

REPRESENTATION, RESPECT AND CULTURAL AWARENESS

In 'We Know the Way', Moana's people sing, 'We tell the stories of our elders / In a never-ending chain.' Given the film's production history, it seems relevant to ask: who is telling the traditional story of these people, and how complicated is it that these stories are being told from outside that 'chain'? Moana's story, which draws heavily on Polynesian culture, is being told through the prism of 'a Disney animated film'. Even though Clements and Musker put together (and took great amounts of guidance from) the Oceanic Story Trust, *Moana* is still an animated fantasy version of Polynesian life and customs steered by two non-Polynesian men. As Vincente M Diaz argues, 'Moana, the Disney film, originates not from Pacific Islander efforts to tell their own stories, but in white male writers actively seeking out raw cultural resources for the Disney machine.'[1]

As an animated studio product, *Moana* also has to fit into the larger Disney business model, which demands profits be made from the film, from the soundtrack and from the merchandising. Indeed, the pressure to make money from the merchandise led to one of the least respectful actions imaginable: a Maui tattooed 'skin-suit' was briefly available as a pull-on child's costume. (It was withdrawn from sale almost immediately as complaints about its offensive nature were made.)

Indeed, Maui's body in the film has been the focus of some intense debate, and is a good example of how Disney's film tangles itself in knots. As Robert Ito points out: 'In illustrated books, comics and animated films, Maui often resembles a lithe teenager on the verge of manhood.'[2] In this movie, Maui has been supersized, partially to make him seem 'god-like' or even perhaps 'superhero-like', and partially to give him a body large enough for his tattoos to be easily 'read'. This representation has led to accusations of Disney perpetuating a comic stereotype about obese Polynesian men instead of depicting this mythic, much-loved Polynesian character in his traditional form.

Despite Disney's desire to make a film that looks beyond mainstream fairytales as its source material, it can't seem to shake off the desire to force characters to conform to conventional visual forms.

- Filmmaking, especially on the scale of a Disney-style animated movie, is an extremely expensive venture. Given the difficulties of getting any story to the screen, what can be done to get more diverse and culturally sensitive stories made?
- Think about the cultural stories of your family or community. Who has the right to tell these stories to a wider audience? Would there be any difficulties if a major movie studio wanted to turn them into a big-budget screen production?
- Imagine that you are in charge of making Disney's next movie project. Based on the success of *Moana*, the studio is planning to make another animated film that is connected to an indigenous culture. What would you suggest could make the movie (and the process of making it) more respectful to the culture that the story originates from?

CONCLUSION

Moana's quest turns out to be both a personal one and a public-interest one. In following her heart, but disobeying her father, Moana uncovers her inner strengths. With the help of Maui, the demigod, and the spirits of her ancestors (including her much-loved Gramma Tala), Moana is able to use those strengths to save her home from destruction and restore the cultural tradition of exploration to her people. Additionally, in searching for ways to tell Moana's story, the creative team and the involvement of the Oceanic Story Trust show us that big-budget animation studios are, while still problematic, capable of moving towards more diverse representation of characters and stories.

Carolyn Leslie is a freelance writer and an IPEd-accredited editor. She also currently teaches in the School of Communication and Creative Arts at Deakin University. You can connect with Carolyn on Twitter @carolynleslie. **SE**

Endnotes

1. Vicente M Diaz, 'Don't Swallow (or be Swallowed by) Disney's "Culturally Authenticated *Moana*"', *Indian Country Today*, 13 November 2016, <https://indiancountrymedianetwork.com/news/opinions/dont-swallow-or-be-swallowed-by-disneys-culturally-authenticated-moana>, accessed 13 April 2017.
2. Robert Ito, 'How (and Why) Maui Got So Big in *Moana*', *The New York Times*, 15 November 2016, <https://www.nytimes.com/2016/11/20/movies/moana-and-how-maui-got-so-big.html?_r=0>, accessed 13 April 2017.

Temporal Truths

THE GIRL WHO LEAPT THROUGH TIME

In this charming feature animation, time travel enables a teenage girl to learn important lessons about life, and about herself. By presenting a narrative that rejects individualism in favour of group harmony, writes SUSAN BYE, Mamoru Hosoda's film also gives Western viewers important insights into Japan's unique culture.

This article refers to the English-dubbed release.

Although *The Girl Who Leapt Through Time* is often classified as science fiction, the most alluring quality of Mamoru Hosoda's 2006 feature animation is its representation of the rhythms of everyday existence. The premise of time travel functions as a narrative device to facilitate protagonist Makoto Konno's (Emily Hirst) discovery of what is important in life, rather than as an opportunity for escape or adventure. Loosely adapting the story told by Yasutaka Tsutsui in his celebrated 1967 book of the same name, Hosoda reimagines it in a twenty-first century context in which 'young people have individual pictures of the future, not collective visions overall'.[1] Hosoda has commented that Tsutsui, who has seen many adaptations of his classic tale, considers Hosoda's film to be a sequel to his story.[2] The basic premise of the original narrative and Hosoda's loose adaptation involves a boy from the future accidentally giving one of his new friends the power to leap back in time. In exploring this idea, Hosoda creates a protagonist whose self-absorption unfixes her from the everyday rhythms of her existence. In resolving this conflict, Makoto develops a more nuanced understanding of community, group harmony and her place in time.

Makoto is a scatterbrained high school student who is determined to avoid any kind of commitment to the future. The film opens with her dreaming of baseball, as she once again sleeps through her alarm and races madly to get to school on time. This routine of haste and disorganisation is so common that her rush to school has become an inconvenient disruption for other commuters who face the same 'ruckus every morning'. On this particular day, Makoto has a series of accidents that includes falling onto a strange walnut-shaped object in the science lab, an event that triggers an intense visionary experience. Makoto's bad day heads towards disaster when her bicycle brakes fail, and she hurtles head over heels into the path of an oncoming train. When she finds herself back on the other side of the barrier and hears the clock chime 4pm for the second time that day, she realises she has been propelled back through time.

Makoto continues on to the Tokyo National Museum, where her aunt (Saffron Henderson), who works as a conservator, is remarkably unsurprised by her niece's story. She comments that it is impossible to reverse time and that, instead, it is Makoto who has gone back in time. Moreover, if she could do it once, there is no reason why she couldn't do it again. Up to this point, Makoto has been characterised by her disinclination to engage dynamically with life. Getting out of bed at the last possible moment is just a symptom of a larger fear about the future, marked by her reluctance to choose an academic stream or to seriously consider a prospective career. Yet, when her aunt suggests that 'time-leaping' is a technique that Makoto can work at and perfect, she is galvanised into action. Tantalised by the chance to move back into the past, she is suddenly filled with energy and resolve.

Poised between the safety of childhood and the responsibilities of adult life, Makoto is prepared to go to any lengths to achieve her goal of going back in time. In the source text, protagonist Kazuko experiences time travel as a 'strange floating sensation', whereas Hosoda's Makoto endures an incredible battering driven by a slapstick energy that adds to the comedy of the film, but also emphasises how desperately committed she is to turning the clock back. It is significant that she is leaping or jumping back in time, rather than 'travelling', as it emphasises the energy and effort that go into this process of propulsion. As Makoto crashes back into the past, the disruption she brings to the physical space around her – books falling in a scattered heap, doors collapsing, cleaning equipment sent flying – also highlights how at odds she is with the rest of her world and its everyday rhythms.

In exploring this idea, Hosoda invests in the mythology of ordinary Japanese life, filling the urban landscape through which Makoto moves with a jumble of houses, shops and street signs. The high school, where much of the narrative is set, is a space that draws on the familiar landscape of everyday life, with its echoey gym, cooking classes, science labs and concrete stairways. Alongside this representation of emblematic Japanese urban life, recognisable landmarks such as the Tokyo National Museum and the busy intersection outside Shibuya railway station reinforce a connection to an idea of real life that is disrupted by Makoto's time-leaping. For those familiar with Tokyo, the view across the river to the busy motorway also fixes the setting as the Shitamachi region of the city, an area that has become connected with a shared nostalgia for the city's disappearing past:

Shitamachi life can be seen as simpler and happier, a more feminine space of community as against the masculine world of corporate life. It is a part of the memory, a place absorbed into the mind and applied anywhere one wants it to be or nowhere it [sic] all.[3]

The landscape of the film is painted in a dreamy colour palette of gentle greens, greys and browns, a slightly faded version of the saturated colours associated with the films of anime auteur Hayao Miyazaki and his production company, Studio Ghibli. Hosoda is determined to find a lyrical beauty in the most mundane of circumstances – a pile of exercise books flying in the air, a student's piano practice, a jelly of glistening gold amid the jumble of the family refrigerator. Hosoda made *The Girl Who Leapt Through Time* in the wake of being replaced as director of Ghibli's *Howl's Moving Castle* (Miyazaki, 2004), and the beauty he infuses into ordinariness poses a kind of challenge to Miyazaki's renowned predilection towards escapism. An exception to this aesthetic of ordinariness is the Konno family's exquisite traditional-style wooden house. Yet the house contains a family very much living in the present, so that the paper screens, polished wood and romantic garden function as evocative reminders of the interconnection between the present and the past.

Initially, much of Makoto's determination to leap back in time is born of self-indulgent and childish desires, such as making sure her sister doesn't eat her pudding, ensuring another chance to eat teppanyaki and engineering a ten-hour-long karaoke session. However, even more seductive is the possibility of changing

events so as to plot a smooth trajectory for herself through the decidedly bumpy world of high school. At this stage of the narrative, Makoto considers the progression of time as purely related to her. Having blitzed the maths quiz she had previously failed, she heads into cooking class and decides to swap cooking stations with the hapless Takase (David Hurwitz) so he has the accident that she had experienced the first time around. But Takase's accident is so much worse: whereas Makoto singes her bangs, Takase causes chaos with a fire extinguisher, incurring the wrath of the school bullies. Takase's accident has prolonged consequences that reverberate through the school community and lead to him losing control of the circumstances he finds himself in and, most shockingly, of his own reactions and responses. As Makoto neatly ties up any of the troublesome loose threads she faces in her life, Takase's life appears to unravel.

As the possibilities of her new power become clear, Makoto begins to imagine herself as invincible; it seems that every hardship or inconvenience can be avoided, and every desire, fulfilled. On the baseball field, she miraculously anticipates each ball that Chiaki (Andrew Francis) hits or pitches, taunting him by announcing, 'There's nothing you can hide from me. I can predict everything you're gonna do. I can beat everyone, every single time.' As she speaks, there is a cut that takes her out of the baseball field and to the top of a hill. Framed from below and in wide shot, her grandiose delusions are accentuated by her maniacal laughter echoing across the landscape. She has clearly succumbed to hubris and, as her overconfidence grows, viewers wait for her to face the inevitable consequences of this kind of arrogance. And, in fact, her smug laughter is going to be checked in the following scene when her aunt asks her if she has ever thought that 'someone might be suffering from [her] good fortune'.

Well before this unsettling (and comic) depiction of Makoto as having been taken over by a deluded fanaticism, we are already in little doubt that she and her behaviour are out of kilter with the world in which she operates. Her attention-seeking and

self-centred behaviour rings warning bells from the beginning, particularly when practised in the context of a culture that places a high value on group harmony and personal restraint. Along with revealing Makoto's uninhibited prescience and good fortune, the karaoke sequence instils a distance between viewer and protagonist. As Makoto executes time-leap after time-leap with obvious delight so as to prolong the karaoke session, Hosoda presents much of the action from the perspective of a pair of imaginary security cameras positioned high on the wall of the booth. By presenting the scene in a manner reminiscent of surveillance footage, feelings of collusion are replaced by a more distanced and critical perspective.[4] After this sequence, Makoto becomes increasingly insensitive and reckless as she uses her power to indulge her every whim, until her aunt reminds her of her responsibility to others.

In a film that works as a series of episodes, the cautionary comment from her aunt leads Makoto in a different but equally risky direction as she focuses on using her power to change circumstances for others. Admiring the courage it took Kaho (Natalie Walters), a nervous younger student, to approach Kōsuke (Alex

Zahara), Makoto becomes determined to get them together, not really acknowledging the impact this might have on the group dynamic and the friendship that Makoto, Kōsuke and Chiaki share. When Chiaki broaches the possibiltity that he and Makoto could go out with each other, seeing as Kōsuke is going to start dating, Makoto begins a desperate series of time-leaps designed to leave Chiaki's words unsaid. Her terror at the prospect that their friendship might change or develop into something else and the energy she commits to preserving the status quo reinforce Makoto's fear of the future.

Makoto's untiring enthusiasm for time-leaping generates enormous comic energy, but viewers are very aware that she is not only tempting fate but also interfering with the seasonal, social and personal rhythms around which human life is organised. In

Chiaki appears to stop time in order to talk to Makoto about who he is, where he has come from and why he has stayed longer than he should have.[5] As the pair walk through a freeze-framed Tokyo, every other person and thing is still in the moment: ball games, children on swings, a clock's pendulum, wine being poured into a glass, fish and birds. A brief glimpse of a cicada just emerged from its carapace recalls the cicadas that have already penetrated the film landscape with their unmistakable sound. Cicadas, which only briefly live above ground, are a traditional symbol of the impermanence of life but, in this frozen tableau, people are just as much a part of this meditation on time and existence.

Chiaki tells Makoto that he stayed because he was having so much fun with her and Kōsuke, but also because he had never seen so many people before. Suspended in time, the families

In Japanese culture, the changing seasons are connected to the idea of impermanence and the transience of human life, and Makoto flouts this understanding each time she tries to change or relive a past event.

Japanese culture, the changing seasons are connected to the idea of impermanence and the transience of human life, and Makoto flouts this understanding each time she tries to change or relive a past event. The human impact of Makoto's time-leaping is obviously expressed via the miserable Takase, but Hosoda also reminds us, through the representation of the summer landscape, that Makoto is tampering with the very essence of life.

The season in which the story is set is communicated through the vibrant green foliage emerging out of the urban landscape, white clouds floating in an azure sky, long days ending in picturesque sunsets, and the deafening chorus of cicadas accompanying the friends' baseball games. The film's depiction of the distinctive cadences of summer culminates in the moment when

at the pool, the businessmen rushing along the street and the crowds making their way across the famous Shibuya crossing are all where they are meant to be, just as the birds making their way across the sky are. To increase the sense of harmony in this scene – a harmony that Makoto is unsettling with her time-leaping – Hosoda has matched shapes to lead us through a world defined by connection: circular shapes give way to swaying shapes, which are linked to water, fish and then to birds. This sequence is poetic in its effect, creating a break in Makoto's frenetic backwards-looking activity, and highlighting the transient and ineffable nature of experience.

Hosoda combines this evocative representation of everyday life with an array of more exaggerated and expressive Japanese animation conventions to communicate information about his characters. In particular, Makoto's vibrant personality and changing moods are denoted through visual iconography: she has the large eyes typically associated with the archetypal *shōjo* character,[6] blushes when embarrassed and sweats when placed under stress. The movement of her hair highlights her youthful energy, her mouth becomes a grotesque hole in the middle of her face when she laughs, and when she cries she spouts a stream of tears. The exaggeration contained in this form of characterisation not only adds to the comedy, but also reflects the intensity of feelings associated with the teenage experience and the transition from the comparative freedom of childhood to the burdens of adult responsibility.

Catherine Driscoll describes 'the contradiction between maturity and immaturity' as 'central to teen film' (which she views in transnational terms)[7] and, by the end of the film, Makoto is very different from the girl at the beginning whose greatest concern was whether her sister had eaten her pudding. Her maturity and wisdom are primarily developed in the popular teen-film setting of the high school, which functions as a liminal space between the worlds of childhood and adult experience. High school culture is typically characterised in the teen-film genre by intense relationships and fixed rules of behaviour that require the young people who inhabit this world to find a balance between their developing senses of self and the demands of the group. Within the context of the Hollywood teen film, the struggle to balance these competing demands of group and individual identity typically involves a rejection of conformity in favour of personal authenticity. By contrast, in *The Girl Who Leapt Through Time*, Makoto must learn to become less self-centred as she focuses on her contribution to the shared experience of the group. Rather than achieving independence, she learns to fit in and make allowances for others, a lesson represented in the baseball game with which the film concludes. Despite the frustration of playing a team sport with inferior players, Makoto has decided to invite Kaho and her friends – novice players – to join her and Kōsuke on the field. As she cheerily watches the girls fumble with the ball, it is clear she has learned to put her wishes and desires to one side in favour of group harmony.

Makoto's newfound patience in the film's present links up with her investment in the future. She has not only promised Chiaki that she will make sure the painting he came back to see will be preserved, but also that she will run to catch up to him in the future. This is a baffling promise, even in terms of the typically fraught logic of time-travel narratives. However, what is most important is Makoto's newly fledged commitment to the future – a commitment reinforced by the image of her head against the brilliant blue of the sky and the casting of her gaze into the clouds. Throughout the film, the sky has stood out as the only space depicted in saturated colour, in contrast to the gentle hues that characterise the rest of the setting. Working as a bookend with Makoto's introduction at the beginning of the narrative, this final image of the sky is a reminder that her future has always been there waiting for her.

Hosoda has stated that a theme common to his films is the human tendency to disconnect from the present: 'People easily ignore what the most important or cherished things are in their day-to-day lives.'[8] The loving depiction of the characters' everyday world is a testament to this idea, but its evocative significance depends on what has gone before and what will follow. The secret to a good life, as Makoto learns, is to create the right balance between the past, the present and the future. The beautiful painting

that has drawn Chiaki to the present day encapsulates this interrelationship. Created long ago during a time of war and famine, the work is being carefully restored by Makoto's aunt in the present and represents Makoto's pledge to Chiaki and the future.

Susan Bye is an Education Programmer at the Australian Centre for the Moving Image. **SE**

Endnotes

1. Mamoru Hosoda, quoted in Ian Condry, *The Soul of Anime: Collaborative Creativity and Japan's Media Success Story*, Duke University Press, Durham & London, 2013, p. 47.
2. See Russell Bekins, '*The Girl Who Leapt Through Time*: Interview with Director Mamoru Hosoda', *Animation World Network*, 21 June 2007, <http://www.awn.com/animationworld/girl-who-leapt-through-time-interview-director-mamoru-hosoda>, accessed 27 February 2017.
3. Paul Waley, 'Moving the Margins of Tokyo', *Urban Studies*, vol. 39, no. 9, August 2002, p. 1548.
4. Hosoda draws attention to this strategy in an interview included as a DVD extra. See 'Interview with Director', *The Girl Who Leapt Through Time*, DVD, Tokikake Film Partners, 2009.
5. In Tsutsui's book, the character from the future also appears to pause time but explains that rather than stopping time, he and Kazuko (the girl who time-leaps) are 'backtracking at exactly the same speed as time is moving forward'. Yasutaka Tsutsui, *The Girl Who Leapt Through Time*, trans. David Karashima, Alma Books, Surrey, UK, 2011 [1967], p. 81.
6. *Shōjo* means 'little female' and describes a set of conventions relating to the representation of young female characters in manga and anime: 'the *shōjo* nestle in a shallow lacuna between adulthood and childhood, power and powerlessness, awareness and innocence as well as masculinity and femininity'. See Tamae Prindle, cited in Susan J Napier, *Anime from Akira to Princess Mononoke: Experiencing Contemporary Japanese Animation*, Palgrave, New York, 2001, p. 119.
7. Catherine Driscoll, *Teen Film: A Critical Introduction*, Berg, Oxford & New York, 2011, p. 2.
8. Mamoru Hosoda, quoted in Chih-Chieh Chang, 'Interview: Mamoru Hosoda, Director of *Wolf Children*', *Anime News Network*, 16 July 2013, <http://www.animenewsnetwork.com/interview/2013-07-15/interview-mamoru-hosoda-director-of-wolf-children>, accessed 27 February 2017.

'I'm a Badass Hunky Dude'

GENDER, HEGEMONY AND *SHE'S THE MAN*

www.screeneducation.com.au

This gender-bending teen film – a loose adaptation of Shakespeare's *The Twelfth Night* – presents many challenges to the status quo, even if it ultimately reinforces mainstream gender norms. ADOLFO ARANJUEZ demonstrates how *She's the Man* can introduce students to ideas about hegemony and, in turn, give them the tools to interrogate the ideologies at play in Hollywood cinema.

Active for a large part of the twentieth century, and largely indebted to the socio-philosophical work of Karl Marx and Georg Wilhelm Friedrich Hegel, the Frankfurt School examined – among other things – the fallibility of capitalism as a politico-economic framework for society as well as the failure of communism to provide a viable alternative. Two of its key theorists, Theodor Adorno and Max Horkheimer, were particularly interested in the way in which what they termed the 'culture industry' perpetuates the societal status quo by bombarding the 'masses' with pop culture products instilled with dominant-group ideology.[1] These views echo the work of neo-Marxist Antonio Gramsci, whose notion of cultural hegemony posits that the lower sectors of society 'consent' to their subordination as they have internalised these ideologies and thus perceive their inferior position as 'natural'.[2]

Hegemony is not static, however, but rather a site of continual conflict. In the case of screen representations of gender, this opposition can be seen in unconventional characters like Viola (Amanda Bynes) from Andy Fickman's 2006 film *She's the Man*. Viola is a soccer aficionado who, disguised as twin brother Sebastian (James Kirk) – they 'look scary-alike', according to his girlfriend, Monique (Alex Breckenridge) – attends his school, Illyria, to join their boys soccer team after her school's girls team is cut. Her characterisation proves subversive in terms of her tomboyish demeanour: not only does she lack interest in typically 'girly' endeavours like shopping and find herself enamoured of a hobby that is traditionally coded as masculine, but she also disdains orthodox notions of feminine demureness. The latter is narratively encapsulated by the local debutante ball, which her mother, Daphne (Julie Hagerty), is obligating her to attend, much to her chagrin: 'I have no interest in being a debutante; it's totally archaic!'

Yet, while counter-hegemonic elements do permeate popular culture, these nevertheless remain secondary to the texts' overall hegemony. Moreover, Adorno and Horkheimer's delineation of a seamlessly top-down relationship between an apparently uniform culture industry and an ultimately passive, subjugated audience oversimplifies what is, in reality, a complex matrix of relationships to do with production and consumption. Nonetheless, examining texts like *She's the Man* in a classroom context gives students the opportunity to engage critically with topics such as sexism, gender norms, patriarchy and heteronormativity, particularly given the high school setting of many teen films aligns with their real-world milieu.

PREVIOUS SPREAD, L–R: Viola (Amanda Bynes) with her 'man', Duke (Channing Tatum); Viola masquerading as her twin brother, Sebastian THIS PAGE, CLOCKWISE FROM TOP LEFT: Viola with soccer teammates Yvonne (Jessica Lucas) and Kia (Amanda Crew); Sebastian (James Kirk); Viola as Sebastian

'GIRLS CAN'T BEAT BOYS'

After learning about her soccer team's dissolution, Viola attempts to reason with her coach (Robert Torti); failing that, she then demands to be allowed to join the boys team in light of her exceptional abilities. But he refuses: 'Girls aren't as fast as boys, or as strong, or as athletic […] it's scientific fact. Girls can't beat boys.' His recourse to 'scientific fact' calls to mind Adorno and Horkheimer's assertion that ideology is effective at concealing its own constructedness. As culture-industry products tend to be composed of interchangeable, formulaic components (such as stereotypical characters and heavily predictable plots) that are peddled time and time again, audiences – in the Frankfurt School schema – eventually lose the ability to recognise that they are being force-fed ideological messages. Men and women get married, women bear children and do the housework, boys will be boys … repetitive representations such as these reassure viewers, through visual catharsis, that their daily travails are 'just the way things are'.[3]

Indeed, gender is arguably the best conduit for Hollywood hegemony. It's worth noting at the outset that Hollywood is an overwhelmingly male-dominated industry,[4] which could plausibly explain the motive to champion patriarchal ideas: by depicting men as powerful and able to wrest their emotions, Hollywood's male moguls are endorsing their suitability for their influential positions.[5] Moreover, in his Master's thesis on Hollywood's depictions of masculinity, Pentti Haddington identifies the consistent alignment of male characters with positive traits like physical strength, avoidance of non-pragmatic verbal communication, and 'proficiency' in sex. These, in turn, are counterposed against 'female' traits – emotionality, vulnerability, a penchant for romance – that, if possessed by a male character, are used as 'evidence' that he is 'not a "real" man',[6] giving rise to 'male hysteria': the demonisation of effeminacy and traits associated with women. Moreover, he notes a number of plot elements that Hollywood often restricts to its male characters, such as avoiding being the object of the 'erotic gaze'.[7]

> It's worth noting at the outset that Hollywood is an overwhelmingly male-dominated industry, which could plausibly explain the motive to champion patriarchal ideas: by depicting men as powerful and able to wrest their emotions, Hollywood's male moguls are endorsing their suitability for their influential positions.

THIS PAGE, CLOCKWISE FROM LEFT: Viola and Sebastian's mother, Daphne (Julie Hagerty); Duke and Viola with Andrew (Clifton Murray) and Toby (Brandon Jay McLaren); a love triangle develops between Olivia (Laura Ramsey), Duke and Viola

The last of these has already been widely studied within feminist film criticism, in particular by Laura Mulvey, who identified the cinematic framing of women as segmented body parts in vertical sequence.[8] Making reference to Freudian theory, she attributes this visual approach – which forms part of a broader objectifying formula whereby female characters are portrayed as subordinate, dependent accessories in chiefly male-driven plotlines – to a patriarchal fear of castration, with men 'suppressing' women by turning them into disempowered objects of voyeurism.[9]

'INSIDE EVERY GIRL, THERE'S A BOY'

As signalled by its title – which juxtaposes the competitive, braggadocious machismo of the common phrase 'the man' with a feminine pronoun – She's the Man revels in turning masculinity on its head. That the film is loosely inspired by William Shakespeare's The Twelfth Night (even featuring characters with the same names) is, therefore, perhaps unsurprising. During the Bard's time, women weren't allowed to perform in the theatre, thereby requiring female roles to be acted by men; in the case of The Twelfth Night's gender-bending deception, the audience is thus treated to a man playing a woman posing as a man. In light of this fact – along with the play's central love triangle, which hints at the blurring of hetero- and homoerotic attraction – it has been noted that the play highlights how gender 'is more like a suit of clothes that can be put on and taken off at will than a matter of biological destiny' and how 'masculinity is a matter of appearances'.[10]

In She's the Man, the idea that gender is performative is well established by the first act. In an early scene, we meet Viola's friend Paul (Jonathan Sadowski), the hairdresser/stylist responsible for her transformation. Even notwithstanding his ambiguous sexual orientation, he works in a 'feminine' industry, dresses flamboyantly in bright colours and behaves in a way that defies the 'masculine' norm. After being told of Viola's plan, he initially warns that she will have trouble getting 'the voice and the mannerisms […] and the mentality' right. Immediately after, we see a 'field research' montage in which Viola shadows various men, closely observing and then imitating their behaviour: she swaggers while walking, stiffens her chest and shoulders, widens her stance, lowers her voice and even – that manliest of actions – hawks up phlegm onto the footpath. Armed with the masculine bravado she attained through mimicry – plus a wig, prosthetic sideburns and a binder to hide her breasts, all courtesy of Paul – Viola in no time convincingly 'transforms' into Sebastian. Soon after arriving at Illyria, Vi-bastian[11] even confronts her momentary self-doubt by invoking the confidence afforded by male privilege: 'I can do this […] I'm a badass hunky dude!'

Vi-bastian's roommate and eventual object of attraction, Duke (Channing Tatum), likewise challenges hegemonic portrayals of masculinity. While he is conventionally attractive, muscular, masculine and the school's top soccer player, he also reveals himself to be what film scholar Jackie Byars refers to as a 'sensitive man' who doesn't fear emotion and is invested in fostering a (female) romantic partner's emotional growth.[12] This aspect of his personality is divulged during several one-on-one conversations between him and Vi-bastian (the frequency of which already undermines the hegemonically masculine aversion to

THIS PAGE, FROM TOP: Yvonne, Kia and Viola with Paul (Jonathan Sadowski); Viola with debutante ball organiser Cheryl (Lynda Boyd); Viola, Olivia, and Sebastian's girlfriend, Monique (Alex Breckenridge)

conversation identified by Haddington). In one scene, he reacts dismissively to Vi-bastian's suggestion that he 'suck it up, be a man and rub some dirt on' a fresh wound. Later, when the pair discover a stray tarantula in their dorm room, they scream together and hug in fear (albeit with the requisite pulling-away dictated by male hysteria because #nohomo). And, when helping Duke decide whether he should date classmate Olivia (Laura Ramsey) or Viola, whom he had met earlier at a town carnival, Vi-bastian's advice to go with which woman Duke 'would rather see naked' is met with ridicule. Duke then protests about Vi-bastian always 'talk[ing] about girls in such graphic terms'. Interestingly, Duke makes the admission that he is 'not really good at talking to girls' – yet the fact that he is able to engage in lengthy banter with Vi-bastian (who, unbeknown to him, *is* female) throws into question the gender-based preconceptions underpinning his statement.

The rest of the film is littered with situational counter-hegemony. In one scene, Illyria principal Horatio Gold (David Cross) reveals that he has worn high heels (footwear that, in recent decades, has been deemed an almost exclusively 'female' item). At a debutante luncheon, jump cuts contrast traditionally feminine Olivia gracefully consuming morsels (accompanied by a non-diegetic flute melody) and 'butchy' Viola gorging on chicken drumsticks (with dopey bassoon music). There, a fight also ensues between Olivia (who has developed romantic feelings for Vi-bastian) and Monique (who accuses Olivia of 'stealing' her boyfriend) – a scenario that, within Hollywood, conventionally occurs when *men* vie for 'possession' of a woman. Moreover, Mulvey's notion of female-as-object is challenged by instances of what E Ann Kaplan calls 'mutual gazing': a tendency for *both* sexes to observe members of the opposite sex.[13] While the majority of objectification scenes in She's the Man involve the male characters ogling the female ones, a key sequence does show Olivia and friend Maria (Katie Stuart) treating Duke and other male students working out at Illyria's gym as attractive men-cum-objects.

'DON'T KICK LIKE A GIRL'

In the film's climax – when Illyria's soccer team face off against their rivals from Viola's school – Vi-bastian's ruse is finally exposed. After some (very problematic) scenes involving Sebastian (who has finally appeared at Illyria) and Viola 'proving' their respective genders by showing some genitals,[14] the rival coach demands that Illyria forfeit, due to the presence of a female player on their team. The Illyria coach (Vinnie Jones) responds by tearing up the soccer-league manual – a delightfully metaphorical visual about *going against the book* – and asserting, 'Here in Illyria, we don't discriminate based on gender.'

At this juncture, we've arrived at the ostensible culmination of She's the Man's revolutionary message against heteronormative, patriarchal dominance: Viola is allowed to play with Illyria, and their team emerges victorious. This girl has beaten everyone by proving she's just as good – or even better – than any boy at soccer. Yet, insidiously, the film's entire arc rests on some contentious ideas. From the very beginning (as indicated by the field-research montage), Viola's masquerade is underpinned by assumptions about what the 'right' type of manhood entails: all of the men she bases her performance on exhibit stereotypically masculine, macho traits. Even dalliances in non-conventional masculinity are quickly subdued within the film – Duke's 'hysterical' response during the tarantula scene exemplifies this, as does the ridiculing of Viola's ex-boyfriend Justin's (Robert Hoffman) crying after losing the soccer match (harking to the still-perpetuated idea that 'boys don't cry').

Viola's masquerade is underpinned by assumptions about what the 'right' type of manhood entails: all of the men she bases her performance on exhibit stereotypically masculine, macho traits.

Other forms of heteronormative prejudice manifest elsewhere in the film. In the narrative's denouement, just before Vi-bastian comes clean, she explains her motivations behind her masquerade then tells Duke, 'Here's the truth: I love you.' Her profession elicits aghast looks and gasps from both teams, her parents and friends, and even the match spectators. While this may be excused in the name of comic relief, it also hints at the idea that same-sex attraction is abnormal – why is it so shocking that Vi-bastian, for all intents and purposes a 'male', could be gay?

At the debutante ball, which Viola eventually agrees to attend despite her date, Duke, failing to turn up, Daphne reassures her, 'You don't need a man to wear a beautiful dress.' On the surface, this may seem like a touching moment between a mother and daughter who have finally reconciled their differing views on womanhood. But this exchange also perpetuates the oppressiveness not just of the commercialistic fashion industry (vis-a-vis the fancy dress), but also of the expectation that women must undergo a 'graceful, ladylike entrée into society', as ball organiser Cheryl (Lynda Boyd) describes it. In light of Viola's earlier protestations about the 'archaic' ceremony and her consistently unashamed dismissal of demureness, we can't help but wonder to what extent her choice to participate in the ceremony is authentic rather than a result of societal pressure.

But the most potent expression of She's the Man's ultimately hegemonic stance comes when Duke and Viola finally reunite towards the end of the film. After some lovey-dovey exchanges that reaffirm the couple's strong feelings for each other, Duke tells Viola that 'from now on in, everything will just be a lot easier if you stayed a girl'. The use of the words 'easier' and 'stayed' quashes any remnants of the film's original position on gender fluidity and performativity. Indeed, here, what is heralded is the notion of gender *essentialism*: Viola, who was 'always' a girl, has finally 'returned' to her rightful state as one, adhering to society's expectation that good girls don pretty dresses and attach themselves to a man. She's the Man closes with a freeze-frame of Duke having caught a jumping Viola – a heteronormative Hallmark-card image if there ever was one.

'SHOW EVERYBODY THE MAN THAT YOU REALLY ARE'

Although entrenched in the realm of hegemony – *She's the Man*, after all, is a Hollywood production and, as such, can be expected to advocate its ideologies – popular culture products indeed possess the potential to be counter-hegemonic. Yet any *counter*-hegemonic elements must, by virtue of being negations, affirm the existence of the sphere of hegemonic control. The incorporative action of hegemony is such that it even co-opts any resistance to prevailing ideologies; as Adorno and Horkheimer put it, 'Departures from the norm are […] calculated mutations which serve […] to confirm the validity of the system'.[15] For hegemony to remain non-coercive, subjugated groups must feel as though changes to their lived realities – in the realm of gender, this spans the growing prominence of feminism, the increasing number of women in sport, and the burgeoning acceptance of trans and non-binary gender identities – have, in some way, been heeded by those in power.

Certainly, the content and structure of films (as *representations* of the real world) are actively shaped by their creators and, as such, are easily instilled with ideologies of one form or another. And, as Hollywood is, fundamentally, a *commercial* institution, it remains centrally preoccupied with selling its products. From this economic mandate arises a pervasive conservatism that rears its head on two interlinked fronts: built into capitalism is an avoidance of risk, relying on modes of production that have already demonstrated financial success; and movies that cater for viewers' extant tastes consistently perform better at the box office, yet these same (male-centric) tastes are constantly shaped by ideologies of subjugation.[16] Whether Hollywood is *intentionally* purveying ideological messages is, of course, impossible to ascertain – a film production involves thousands of employees, both on and off screen, each working with a multiplicity of aims and motivations. Nevertheless, the overarching goal of maximising revenue – via 'safe' formulas and by tapping into existing audience tastes – leads to the (perhaps inadvertent) outcome of hegemonic dominance.[17]

> Although entrenched in the realm of hegemony – *She's the Man*, after all, is a Hollywood production and, as such, can be expected to advocate its ideologies – popular culture products indeed possess the potential to be counter-hegemonic.

Ultimately, however, we need to bear in mind that exposure to oppositional views can be beneficial in the long run. Although *She's the Man* ends with a Hollywood happy ending that promotes the patriarchy, the fact that the film has also included portrayals of unorthodox characters and situations is, arguably, constructive. Here, the importance of active viewing and media literacy – and the problematic assumptions of the Frankfurt School – are brought to significant attention. Media Studies continually (and justifiably) debunks the soundness of the 'hypodermic needle' communication theory, which envisages a passive audience 'injected' with dominant-culture ideology by a uniform mass media,[18] as, in reality, the meanings of Hollywood films (and texts in general) are always subject to audience interpretation. It's imperative, therefore, that viewers – younger ones especially – be equipped with the tools to critique hegemonic depictions *and* decode counter-hegemonic representations such as those in *She's the Man*.

It cannot be denied that within popular culture rages a battle for ideological supremacy. The Frankfurt School seem correct in regarding popular culture as replete with ideological meanings – Hollywood films are a testament to this – but there is merit to be gained from having both hegemonic and counter-hegemonic elements within popular culture texts. It is through the former that the latter are able to disseminate viewpoints that interrogate the status quo. As Haddington proclaims, 'the more there are cracks [in hegemonic representations], the more society may change'.[19]

Viola and Duke get their hegemonic 'happy ending'

https://clickv.ie/w/screen-ed/shes-the-man

Adolfo Aranjuez is the editor of Metro, *the subeditor of* Screen Education, *and a freelance writer, speaker and dancer. He has edited for* Voiceworks *and* Melbourne Books, *and been published in* Right Now, The Lifted Brow, The Manila Review, Eureka Street *and* Peril, *among others. Adolfo is one of the Melbourne Writers Festival's 30 Under 30. <http://www.adolfoaranjuez.com>* **SE**

Endnotes

1. Theodor Adorno & Max Horkheimer, 'The Culture Industry: Enlightenment as Mass Deception', *Dialectic of Enlightenment*, 2005 [1944], trans. Andy Blunden, available at Marxists Internet Archive, <https://www.marxists.org/reference/archive/adorno/1944/culture-industry.htm>, accessed 18 March 2017.
2. Stuart Hainsworth, 'Gramsci's Hegemony Theory and the Ideological Role of the Mass Media', *Mass Media*, 17 May 2000.
3. Dominic Strinati, *An Introduction to Theories of Popular Culture*, 2nd edn, Routledge, London, 2004, pp. 61–2.
4. Manohla Dargis, 'In Hollywood, It's a Men's, Men's, Men's World', *The New York Times*, 24 December 2014, <https://www.nytimes.com/2014/12/28/movies/in-hollywood-its-a-mens-mens-mens-world.html>, accessed 18 March 2017.
5. Pentti Haddington, '"This Is Not Going to Have a Happy Ending": Searching for New Representations of Hollywood Masculinities in David Fincher's *Se7en*', Master's thesis, Department of English, University of Oulu, May 1998, pp. 18–24.
6. ibid., p. 16.
7. ibid., pp. 26–7.
8. Laura Mulvey, 'Visual Pleasure and Narrative Cinema', *Visual and Other Pleasures*, Macmillan, London, 1989 [1975], pp. 19–21.
9. ibid., pp. 14–5
10. Bruce R Smith, quoted in Miranda Fay Thomas, 'A Queer Reading of *Twelfth Night*', *Discovering Literature: Shakespeare and Renaissance Writers*, British Library website, <https://www.bl.uk/shakespeare/articles/a-queer-reading-of-twelfth-night>, accessed 18 March 2017.
11. For expedience, this piece will use the name 'Vi-bastian' to refer to the character of Viola masquerading as Sebastian.
12. Jackie Byars, 'Gazes/Voices/Power: Expanding Psychoanalysis for Feminist Film and Television Theory', in E Deidre Pribram (ed.), *Female Spectators: Looking at Film and Television*, Verso, London, 1988, p. 118.
13. E Ann Kaplan, cited in ibid., p. 124.
14. The catchcry 'genitals do not equal gender' has gained increasing currency in recent decades, as part of the growing recognition of non-cisgender equality; for more on this, listen to non-binary genderqueer advocate Hollie Howitt's views in 'Genitals Do Not Equal Gender', Joy FM, 2 February 2015, <https://joy.org.au/wetspot/2015/02/02/genitals-do-not-equal-gender/>, accessed 18 March 2017.
15. Adorno & Horkheimer, op. cit., p. 355.
16. See Dargis, op. cit.; and Hannah Shaw-Williams, 'Is There a Formula for Box Office Success?', *Screen Rant*, 28 October 2015, <http://screenrant.com/star-wars-box-office-success/>, accessed 18 March 2017.
17. Richard Maltby, *Harmless Entertainment: Hollywood and the Ideology of Consensus*, The Scarecrow Press, Metuchen, NJ, 1983, pp. 24–5.
18. See David Morley, 'Audience Research', Museum of Broadcast Communications website, <http://www.museum.tv/eotv/audiencerese.htm>; and Brett Lamb, 'Communication Theories', *lessonbucket*, 28 April 2013, <http://lessonbucket.com/vce-media/units-3-4/media-influence/communication-theories/>, both accessed 18 March 2017.
19. Haddington, op. cit., p. 34.

CINEMA SCIENCE

Cinema Science is an ongoing column that explores how cinema – particularly popular, contemporary cinema – employs science and mathematics concepts. In each instalment, DAVID CREWE will explore how movies can help facilitate learning in STEM subjects.

www.screeneducation.com.au

Passengers and the Specifics of Space

First up: 2016 Hollywood space blockbuster *Passengers*. Just how realistic is this depiction of interplanetary travel? Is it possible for humans to hibernate? Could you really grow a forest in a spaceship? And why is Jennifer Lawrence's hair immune to zero gravity?

The erosion of the monoculture can make things tricky for a secondary school teacher looking to build student engagement by digging into pop culture. Take any sizeable group of teenagers and it's hard to find anything they'll all be intimately familiar with. Some might use Facebook obsessively; others might have never made an account. Some students might obsess over the Marvel Cinematic Universe; others might not know the difference between Captain America and Captain Marvel. This student plays videogames obsessively; that student is subscribed to hundreds of YouTube channels.

While cinema's cultural domination might have faded long ago, it's a safe bet that most of your students will have watched *a* movie in the recent past. Cinema Science is aimed at science and/or mathematics teachers looking to leverage modern movies into (hopefully) more engaging lessons, and as such will generally focus on prominent movies – with big budgets, big stars and big box office receipts. You can't guarantee that all your students will have seen the films I'll focus on in this column, but with any luck they'll at least be aware of them.

Which brings us to this issue's focus: 2016 Hollywood movie *Passengers* (Morten Tyldum). While not exactly a blockbuster, the film – which can be described as something between speculative sci-fi and romantic comedy – performed well in Australia, likely thanks to its high-profile stars, Chris Pratt and Jennifer Lawrence.

The film also earnt its fair share of controversy thanks to its dubious ethical underpinning. *Passengers*, set some time in the future, takes place on *Avalon*, a spaceship hurtling towards a distant, uninhabited planet. Everyone aboard is supposed to be in suspended animation for the duration of the journey – some 120 years – but Jim Preston (Pratt) is woken up far too early by an asteroid-impelled glitch. Driven to desperation by his solitude, he ends up awakening Aurora Lane (Lawrence) for company, a plot point conveniently concealed by the film's marketing. Many critics have attacked the film for implicitly excusing, even endorsing, Jim's reprehensible actions.[1]

Passengers undoubtedly opens up rich questions regarding ethics and gender, but my emphasis here is what the film offers to science and mathematics teachers. While the film's focus is on character, the spaceship setting accommodates some in-depth consideration of space travel that opens up ideas relating to human biology, gravity, fluid mechanics and communicating in space. The film is best suited to senior science classes (Year 10 and up) both due to its M classification and the complexity of its associated scientific concepts.

SUSPENDED ANIMATION

The characters' journey to distant solar systems is made possible by a familiar science fiction concept: suspended animation. This acts as a solution to the problem of interplanetary travel in a universe that's, frankly, just too damn big. Where plenty of settings rely on faster-than-light travel – *Star Wars*' hyperspace, *Star Trek*'s warp speed – suspended animation offers a more realistic, if more narratively challenging, answer to traversing distances of many light-years.

Suspended animation features across a range of sci-fi universes. From *Lost in Space* to *Alien* (Ridley Scott, 1979), *2001: A Space Odyssey* (Stanley Kubrick, 1968) to *Interstellar* (Christopher Nolan, 2014), audiences are accustomed to stars taking an extended nap as part and parcel of their space adventures. *Passengers* feels like a natural reaction to the ubiquity of the device, asking a simple question – 'What if you woke up too early?' – to an audience very comfortable with the idea. It seems reasonable to expect that even if your students have yet to see *Passengers*, they'll know what you're talking about when it comes to suspended animation and space travel.

The big question for science classrooms: is it realistic? Well, if we want to talk about the way it is depicted in this film, even the screenwriter, Jon Spaihts, acknowledges that, no, it isn't:

I looked at a lot of ways of potentially putting people to sleep for space, and there, as in many places in sci-fi screenwriting, I ran into tensions between the dramatic requirements of the film and hard science. Our best bet for putting people down right now would be either an extreme therapeutic hypothermia or a freezing process coupled with the development of some perfect cell-by-cell antifreeze to prevent ice crystal rupture of tissue. None of those things are real sexy to wake up from. None of those are states in which Sleeping Beauty in her bed would look particularly gorgeous.[2]

If we disregard the cosmetic realities of Hollywood filmmaking, there's a wealth of discussion points for the Biology classroom. It allows for a considered discussion of animal hibernation, and whether or not the same principles could reasonably apply to human anatomy. By focusing on freezing,[3] one can examine the limits of human endurance, and the chemical challenges of, as Spaihts suggests, ice crystals rupturing cellular membranes. (Also a good opportunity to remind your students not to re-freeze thawed food.)

This isn't a purely theoretical debate, either! A significant challenge facing modern astronomical engineers is how to safely transport astronauts to and from Mars, and suspended animation – of a sort – has the potential to be an efficient solution. A recent paper presented at a NASA symposium found that placing astronauts in 'an inactive, torpor state for the duration of the in-space mission segments' through therapeutic hypothermia could 'double the number of crew members for the same habitat mass'.[4] While century-long sleeps are a long way off, artificial hibernation has a lot of potential in the near future as a way to conserve energy and expense in space travel.

> Most movies opt for the easy solution of 'artificial gravity' with no particular attempt at an explanation, but *Passengers* offers a more robust – if not especially explicit – solution to simulating gravity in the empty expanse of space: centripetal force.

- How does hibernation differ, biologically, from sleeping?
- What benefits are there to suspending animation in space travel – whether travelling to distant planets, or within our own solar system? Is the representation of suspended animation seen in popular films (like *Passengers*) realistic?
- Is it feasible to 'unfreeze' a cryogenically frozen organism? What are the associated challenges, and how might they vary for different organisms?
- How does therapeutic hypothermia work? What risks are associated with the technique?

ARTIFICIAL GRAVITY

The immensity of the universe – and the time taken to traverse it – poses many problems. But so too does the *absence* of something: gravity. Human bodies accustomed to Earth's gravity are ill prepared for extended exposure to zero gravity. Muscles atrophy; bones weaken. Nor are these issues easily addressed by conventional solutions like, say, regular exercise to simulate the influence of gravity. NASA observes that '[s]pace flight may result in changes to muscle metabolism […] that can not be counteracted with routine exercise'.[5] Even one's skeleton erodes under microgravity: 'Bones lose calcium […ND] the skeletal system becomes weaker and less capable of withstanding the stresses associated with daily life on Earth.'[6]

The importance of these problems becomes literally astronomical when long-term space flight is taken into account, like, say, a 120-year journey to a distant solar system. More practically, it's a logistical nightmare to try and set a movie entirely in zero gravity[7] (somewhat ironically, Alfonso Cuarón's 2013 film *Gravity* is the only example I can think of). Most movies opt for the easy solution of 'artificial gravity' with no particular attempt at an explanation, but *Passengers* offers a more robust – if not especially explicit – solution to simulating gravity in the empty expanse of space: centripetal force.

Centripetal force is the force acting on any object travelling in a circle, directed towards the centre of the circle. In practice, if you spin a spacecraft at the right speed, passengers will experience acceleration pushing them towards the centre of motion that roughly approximates a gravitational field. There's no explicit explanation of this within *Passengers*' diegesis, but given that *Avalon* is consistently shown revolving at a constant speed *except* when the gravity fails, it's a reasonable conclusion to draw.[8]

The underlying concepts and mathematics of such simulation provide a rich vein for Physics teachers. Students could independently explore how such systems might operate; the spinning-water-in-a-bucket trick is a good way to see the phenomenon in practice. They could also look into the drawbacks associated with this methodology, such as the Coriolis effect, or specifically investigate whether or not *Passengers* represents the phenomenon realistically. For example, by watching an exterior

shot of the spacecraft and timing the period of rotation, students could – with a few approximations and assumptions – determine the size *Passengers*' ship would need to be to reasonably simulate the Earth's gravity.

As with suspended animation, these applications aren't relegated to the world of speculative fiction. While there's yet to be a real-world space project to substantially incorporate centripetal concepts to simulate gravity, a number of proposals – such as the Nautilus-X[9] – have included such features in their design. There's plentiful potential for tasks built around how different engineers have proposed to address the challenges of artificial gravity for the future of space travel.

- Given the period of rotation of *Passengers*' spacecraft, how large would the ship have to be to convincingly approximate the Earth's gravity?

- When the gravity fails in the film, the ship's rotation swiftly comes to a halt. Is this a realistic outcome?[10]
- Aurora almost drowns in the swimming pool as the water forms bubbles without gravity to keep it in the pool. Is this how you would expect fluid to act in zero gravity? Would there be any way for her to escape from the water without gravity?
- Other than centripetal force, how could one simulate gravity in outer space?

SPEEDING THROUGH SPACE

Suspended animation and artificial gravity are science fiction (and, potentially, science fact) solutions to the problem of how to sustain human life on an intergalactic voyage. But the challenges of space travel go beyond how to survive the trip: the larger question is, simply, how do we even get there?

The challenges of space travel go beyond how to survive the trip: the larger question is, simply, how do we even get there?

That's clearly a question on the mind of Spaihts, who again endeavoured to keep as closely as possible to realistic science. Where, as discussed, many fictional universes rely on faster-than-light travel expressly forbidden by our laws of physics, *Avalon* has 'no warp drive', nor can it go into hyperspace.[11] While these particulars aren't discussed within the film proper – despite being

an engineer himself, Pratt's character is more interested in his personal predicament than how his home-turned-tomb gets from A to B – they have the potential to open up a range of discussion points for Physics students.

For starters, there's the logistics of space travel. To travel long distances requires a source of energy, and the most efficient sources of energy – fossil fuels – take up a not-insignificant amount of room and, more pressingly, mass on board a spaceship. The further you want to travel, the more fuel you need, which means you're carrying more weight, which means you need more fuel … and so on and so on, even without considering the necessary gear needed to account for repairs and sustenance. A task structured around these challenges would help students to recognise that resourcing is a significant real-world limitation on any scientific innovation.

Of course, the real underlying challenge is the sheer size of the universe. Students could explore nearby systems and the distances to them – invariably measured in light-years – to understand the scale of space. Once we narrow our criteria to planets that might potentially sustain life (more on this later), the distances become even more immense. This also opens up the opportunity to investigate how we know the distance to remote interstellar bodies – a convenient segue, perhaps, into spectroscopy, Hubble's law and the big bang theory.

At the upper end of secondary school science, these conversations could also incorporate an inquiry into *why* spaceships are unable to accelerate faster than the speed of light. Relativity – both special and general – could be naturally included in an astrophysics unit centring on concepts relating to the origin and scale of the universe.

Admittedly, concepts of relativity are quite a few steps removed from *Passengers* itself. An investigation that could be linked more explicitly to the film and its depiction of interspace travel is to determine how fast *Avalon* is supposed to be moving. When Jim attempts to send an SOS message back to Earth, he's

shown that it would take over a decade for that transmission to reach Earth, and even longer for the reply to come. If we assume that these messages are transmitted as radio waves, and therefore at the speed of light, it would be relatively trivial for students to approximate the velocity of the spaceship.

- Research the maximum speed a man-made spacecraft has been able to achieve in space. At this speed, how long would it take for us to reach nearby solar systems / galaxies?
- One of the primary restrictions on long-distance interstellar travel is fuel. Can you think of any ways that this problem could be resolved?
- Why can't spaceships like *Avalon* simply accelerate to faster than the speed of light to travel to distant planets?

ODDS AND ENDS

The previous three topics are built around extended classroom tasks, whether for assessment or otherwise, on the assumption a teacher might need to take time out from normal class activities to show the entirety of *Passengers*. However, the film also offers potential for smaller learning experiences built around clips or concepts rather than the entire movie.

For example, in light of NASA's recent discovery of 'seven Earth-size planets around a single star' in the Aquarius constellation,[12] one could branch off from *Passengers*' trip to a habitable exoplanet to consider the question of how scientists could identify such planets. Or, instead, classes could discuss the necessary conditions for sustaining life – a topic that incorporates chemistry (What does it mean to be a carbon-based life form? What temperature does a planet need to be to have liquid water?), biology (What are the necessary conditions for a biosphere to form? How does complex life evolve from single-celled creatures?) and geology (What materials would a planet need to consist of to be sufficiently stable to support the evolution of life?).

Robotics, a relatively new branch of learning in many schools, could also benefit from using *Passengers* as stimulus material. The film features a very advanced take on artificial reality in Michael Sheen's robot bartender, Arthur. But it also includes more rudimentary robots, like the remote-controlled device that Jim uses to ask Aurora out on their first date. The latter could be a

goal for a robotics class to work towards: a robot that can deliver a message to someone just like in the movie.

There's even the unlikely pairing of the film with agricultural science, despite its extraterrestrial setting. How, exactly, is Jim able to successful grow a tree – and, eventually, an entire forest – within the confines of a metal-plated spaceship? Essentially, what are the environmental requirements for plant life, and is it realistic that these requirements would be met on a closed spaceship?

For all the educational potential of *Passengers*, it is important to note that the ethical questions raised – particularly those of consent – are almost certain to come up if the entire film is screened for a class. Whether or not a teacher wishes to engage in an extended discussion on the topic will likely vary from person to person, but given the controversial nature of the film's 'romance', it's something worth carefully considering before screening the film.

David Crewe is a secondary school teacher and freelance writer based in Brisbane, Queensland. He shares his reviews and ruminations on his own website, ccpopculture, *and has been published by SBS Movies,* Metro *magazine,* The Guardian *and* The Big Issue. **SE**

Endnotes

1. Rebecca Hawkes, 'Chris Pratt and Jennifer Lawrence's *Passengers* Isn't a Romance: It's a Creepy Ode to Manipulation', *The Telegraph*, 16 December 2016, <http://www.telegraph.co.uk/films/2016/12/16/chris-pratt-jennifer-lawrences-passengers-isnt-romance-creepy/>, accessed 15 February 2017.
2. Jon Spaihts, quoted in Sheila Roberts, '*Passengers*: 8 Things to Know About the Science Behind the Space Drama', *Collider*, 20 December 2016, <http://collider.com/passengers-movie-things-to-know-jon-spaihts/>, accessed 15 February 2017.
3. Another common trope, whether in *Captain America: The First Avenger* (Joe Johnston, 2011), stories about Walt Disney or even *Encino Man* (Les Mayfield, 1992). (Alright, it's probably unreasonable to expect your students to have heard about that last one.)
4. John Bradford, *Torpor Inducing Transfer Habitat for Human Stasis to Mars*, SpaceWorks Enterprises, Inc. and NASA Innovative Advanced Concepts, May 2014, available at <http://www.sei.aero/eng/papers/uploads/archive/NIAC_SpaceTorpor_Report_May2014_ExecutiveSummary.pdf>, accessed 23 March 2017, pp. 2, 3.
5. 'Maintaining Strength in Space: Bone, Muscle, and Metabolic Studies', The NASA Shuttle Web, 24 October 1998, <https://spaceflight.nasa.gov/shuttle/archives/sts-95/factsheets/fs1998_09_009jsc.html>, accessed 20 February 2017.
6. ibid.
7. Beyond the budget for visual effects, every actor needs a crew cut – realistically simulating the motion of hair in zero gravity is incredibly difficult unless you actually film the scenes in freefall, as in *Apollo 13* (Ron Howard, 1995).
8. There's extratextual evidence to support this interpretation: Spaihts describes the ship as having no artificial gravity in Roberts, op. cit.
9. Details on the Nautilus-X can be found at Jonathan O'Callaghan, 'Nautilus-X: The Multi-purpose NASA Spacecraft That Could Take Humans to the Moon and Beyond', *Space Answers*, 14 January 2014, <https://www.spaceanswers.com/futuretech/nautilus-x-the-multi-purpose-nasa-spacecraft-that-could-take-humans-to-the-moon-and-beyond/>, accessed 24 February 2017.
10. In short: no. For starters, the angular momentum of the ship – and the presumed lack of any significant friction in space – would mean that it would take an awfully long time to come to a stop and thereby return the passengers to zero 'gravity'. Equally, the film's sequencing of events suggests that the failure of the gravity causes the ship to stop spinning, rather than the other way around.
11. Spaihts, quoted in Roberts, op. cit.
12. 'NASA Telescope Reveals Largest Batch of Earth-size, Habitable-zone Planets Around Single Star', media release, NASA, 23 February 2017, <https://www.nasa.gov/press-release/nasa-telescope-reveals-largest-batch-of-earth-size-habitable-zone-planets-around>, accessed 25 February 2017.

Kids on Film
Teaching Documentary in the English Classroom

Far from the dry, didactic texts they are sometimes dismissed as, documentaries have the power to engage teenagers in a way that most other media don't, as the form increasingly overlaps with young people's own documentation and presentation of life via social media. LOUISE LAVERY outlines a unit she developed and executed that resulted in her Year 9 English students understanding, and wholly embracing, nonfiction cinema.

www.screeneducation.com.au

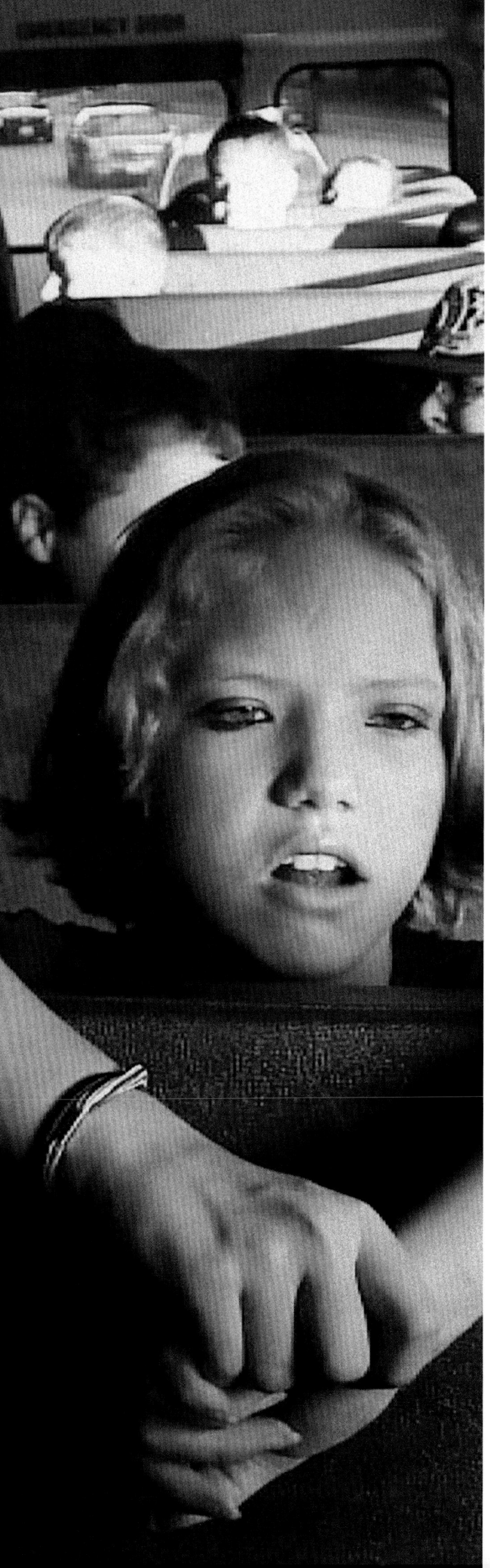

SCREENS IN THE CLASSROOM

MY

The place of documentaries in English classrooms has a rich history. This form provides educators with a cache of excellent source material that allows students to access a range of reader and analytical perspectives that they may not have seen before. The documentary turns the classroom into a hotbed of inquiry where a plethora of biased viewpoints are waiting to be unpacked by minds coming to terms with the idea of looking outside themselves and their own experiences in order to engage with the complex world around them. It is this very access to the broader world, this opportunity to push students beyond passivity and towards questioning and critical analysis, that can ignite excitement in the teacher who sees such an area of study approaching in their syllabus. They plan and prepare with rigour and excitement, determined that they will be the one to spark the sense of wonderment and awe that so often accompanies the viewing of such constructed truths in the developing minds of their students. They create intricate lessons wherein they unpack theory and technique, envisaging the disinterested teens under their care suddenly awakening and rising to stand on their desks *Dead Poets*–style in recognition of the teacher who finally got them to look up from their iPhones to see the people around them. O Captain! My Captain!

That is, of course, until they are met with the soul-crushing cries of 'This is boring!' and 'Why are we doing this?' and 'Can I go to the toilet?' It is here that the classroom teacher will often falter, stumble over a few worksheets and then ultimately just chuck on something by Michael Moore and ask students to write a review. They will cry to their Facebook feed about today's teenagers being lost causes who are too absorbed in themselves to care about anyone else. Alas, poor documentary study. We knew him well.

Sort of.

To understand how best to teach the documentary in English classrooms, it is useful to first recognise the ways in which your students are already interacting with the artform in their own lives. This is a generation of media consumers who are carefully curating their own versions of reality using tools like Snapchat and Instagram. Savvy teen producers of online content in these bite-size forms are mapping together their own digital identities and offering unique lenses on their lived experiences. Their audiences can be wide and varied so their messages become carefully tailored, and they use many of the same techniques we see in film to portray themes and ideas specific to their lives. Concern over teenagers using social media generally only paints this use as problematic and immature; what is missing from this understanding is the idea that these young people are producers of media who are making very careful decisions and filtering their versions of reality for the consumption of others. As a result, studying documentary can be the perfect fit, as many of the children in our classrooms are already developing their own commentaries on the world around them.

As educators, and as adults, we often underestimate the degree to which our students are already engaged as social citizens. It's all too easy to believe the hype that this generation of teenagers is incredibly selfish and introverted due to an over-reliance on technology (that we gave them) and not going out into the world as much as we did (because we destroyed it for them). Teenagers are often positioned as placid, doughy and uncaring parasites focused on nothing more than superficialities and no-holds-barred consumerism.[1] Our society seems to both mock and shame teenagers in equal measure. These young people, who are merely operating

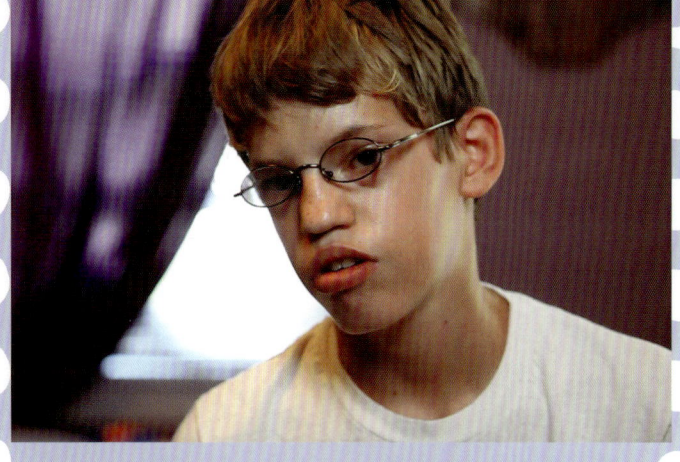

PREVIOUS SPREAD AND ABOVE: *Bully*

within the frame of reference that we have created for them, are heavily criticised and parodied as immature (think Jimmy Fallon's 'Ew' segment on *The Tonight Show*) while being completely objectified and oversexualised (case in point being the media's negative focus on Kylie Jenner[2] and social media stars of her ilk), to the extent that we see them as caricatures and forget that these are individuals looking for their place in the world.

And it's the 'finding relevance' part that's absolutely crucial in terms of students making a connection with anything we try and do. As educators of English and film, we cannot assume that because we find merit in a particular text, it means students, of sometimes vastly different cultural and socio-economic backgrounds than us, will as well. It is easy to forget that when we were students ourselves, we were often just as bored as the teenagers sitting in front of us now. We were just as disengaged from what our teachers considered to be classic texts as our own students are with the content that we're expecting them to engage with.

A unit about documentary that includes the element of student choice and evaluation has proven to be an effective way to overcome some of these issues. The following case study concerns an English unit taught to a Year 9 cohort at an independent girls college in Brisbane. In it, students were given the opportunity to learn about the form and then apply their learning by making appraisals about a filmmaker's intentions and whether or not their objective – to connect with their intended audience – was achieved.

* * *

This unit of work had a very specific context. Students were to deliver a seminar presentation to an imagined external body, outlining the reasons why other Year 9 English students should study a particular documentary in their second semester. Framing the unit thusly allowed students to explore aspects of the genre from an active, almost scientific perspective, as they knew they would have to apply this learning and theory to their analytical exposition. They would be asked to link the film text itself to its authorship, intended audience, invited readings and, more broadly, to the social world by means of unpacking how the techniques elected to tell this story connected (or did not connect) with a teenage audience.

Most teachers in a typical English department won't have media, film and/or television training or experience. This is not

It is easy to forget that when we were students ourselves, we were often just as bored as the teenagers sitting in front of us now. We were just as disengaged from what our teachers considered to be classic texts as our own students are with the content that we're expecting them to engage with.

These very ideas of autonomy, self-awareness and relevance are present in students' online stories, and they should be underpinning educational approaches to dealing with documentaries in the English classroom. Not to be confused with the reality television genre, which sells audiences a particular product via a highly constructed narrative based on often-negative archetypes, long-form documentary holds many opportunities for students to develop stronger critical and analytical skills that can later be employed in the senior syllabus. The curriculum holds a lot of room for creative engagement with and exploration of film texts, but this is often limited to a study of fictional narratives – looking at old texts like *Stand by Me* (Rob Reiner, 1986) that are just nostalgic explorations for the teacher instead of meaningful texts that today's students can find relevance in.

necessarily an indication that they cannot teach these text forms, but it often means that they are intrinsically reluctant because they fear that they may not be doing it 'correctly' – whatever that means. Any teacher worth their salt will tell you that a film is just as valid a text as a novel or a play – a glimpse at the list of any external senior English exam will show you the breadth of film texts available to study. This is not just the realm of the review task or the 'Friday-arvo fill-in' – encourage your colleagues to upskill and become familiar with production terminology so that they can enhance their own practice.

Getting a departmental grasp on the language associated with the film form is the first step to ensuring a consistent message for students. In the case of the school in question, this language was best delivered to students in the form of a lecture given by an experienced teacher of Media who was also an English teacher (and who was also, in the interest of full disclosure, me). In terms of professional development and cross-curricular approaches, sharing resources like this can be determined as best practice in the collegial sense, as well as promoting an atmosphere of academic rigour and high expectations. Students attended a university-style lecture on the constructed nature of film techniques and found themselves engaged in higher-order thinking practices, trying to determine the answers to questions surrounding a filmmaker's choice to use contrapuntal sound, or a cinematographer's preference for wide-angle lenses. As all students experienced this information at the same time as a group, teachers were able to follow up on it in the classroom without the dreaded cry of 'But the other class didn't do this!' that can so often get in the way of trying to best tailor content for the individuals in front of you.

The lecture came after teachers spent a number of weeks leading their students through some introductory documentary activities. Media teachers often understand the value of immersing students in a new genre before asking them to comment on it, but English teachers may not be aware that it actually is best to allow for a lot of viewing to take place in the orientation phase of a unit on a film that the cohort is unfamiliar with. My class, for example, viewed a number of short documentaries like *The Boy Who'll Never Grow Up* (a fairly standard observational documentary with an emotive narrative, which aired on ABC2 in 2015), *Grey Gardens* (Albert Maysles et al., 1975; a cult documentary to explore the world of cinema vérité) and the ever-popular *Super Size Me* (Morgan Spurlock, 2004). I held screening lessons in our double periods (Wednesdays). I found it best to talk about the various documentary styles prior to viewing, have students do some background reading at home in the lead-up to the screening so they had a frame of reference, screen the film and then ask them to document their thoughts that evening as to how it did (or did not) connect with their teenage experience.

Beyond the screenings of the documentary films I had selected, my class also worked quite closely with the content in the 'Documentary' section of the Short of the Week website.[3] This is an excellent resource because not only does it have a very wide variety of subject matter, but any inappropriate content is very clearly flagged so a younger audience can avoid it (and so you can cover yourself in case they do become overly adventurous). My students constructed a few basic reviews of these films as well as a range of group and individual presentation tasks whereby they tried to apply a higher-level form of engagement. Groups explored what the filmmakers wanted to do with their films, how they went about it and whether or not students felt they were successful. Prompting the students to continuously engage with these films through writing, conversation and presentation meant we were able to move past their expectation that films are primarily meant to entertain, and towards a deeper understanding of the power of documentaries to question, challenge, engage and explore.

The idea of flipped learning inspired my approach to having students pre-read the classroom content. Unit orientation activities that draw on students' prior knowledge really only work if there is any prior knowledge to connect with – otherwise it can be an exercise in students claiming that something is boring and questioning its place in a field of study. Arming students with knowledge prior to discussion puts them in the mindset of being mini-experts who are capable of grasping broader concepts rather than feeling they had to passively wait to be told what to think by their teacher.

Grey Gardens

Armed with knowledge, content, interest and prior experience in terms of film analysis, students set about selecting their documentaries for their seminar presentation. A lot of consideration was given to the parameters of this task. It was agreed that, due to the young age of these students, a PG rating would be our target. Students were permitted to study something of a more advanced rating as long as we obtained written permission from their parents and any content delivered in their seminar was still classroom-appropriate. This offered a wider scope of material for students to work with and included many of their parents in their learning as well – a pleasant outcome for any task.

Once the theoretical content and the whole-class viewing had taken place, I modelled a presentation for my students based on one of the films we had seen, Spurlock's *Super Size Me*. Teaching can often be an exercise in frustration when we attempt to get

FROM TOP: *Blackfish* (two images); *Sherpa* (two images)

suddenly became their whole world as they sought to attach significance to what they were seeing. Their capacity for critical engagement and literacy leapt as the students refused to let content passively pass them by and instead questioned whether the use of animation, for example, was for comedic or manipulative effect. Seeing girls of this age, who are so often criticised and dismissed as selfish and silly, so excited about what they were doing and the connections that they were making was more than a little inspiring. This task gave them the tools to pull something apart and put it back together again – something it seems students are not often expected or encouraged to be able to do.

The presentations themselves were incredibly rewarding from my perspective as an English teacher, a Media teacher and a feminist. They embraced a creative structure that sought to deliver the world of the film to the audience in a neat little four-minute package. Girls spoke with passion and enthusiasm about the intended messages behind films like *Blackfish* (Gabriela Cowperthwaite, 2013), *Sherpa* (Jennifer Peedom, 2015), *That Sugar Film* (Damon Gameau, 2014), *9/11: The Falling Man* (Henry Singer, 2006) and *Bully* (Lee Hirsch, 2011). They explored the relevance of expository, observational and cinema vérité forms to a young audience and reflected on the process of meaning-making in visual texts. My feedback paragraphs were filled with points like 'masterful control over metalanguage', 'excellent analysis of the presence of both non-diegetic and contrapuntal music' and 'sophisticated understanding of audience response to invited reading'. The students made connections between interview subjects speaking

The students made connections between interview subjects speaking directly to the camera and YouTube and Vine stars who can make quick but lasting connections with their audiences.

students to guide themselves through tasks that we completely understand but that they may never have encountered before. As we were asking students to make connections between a film text, the intention of its creators, invited readings and how a young audience could potentially find resounding truth and connection, it was important that students see a working example of how their exposition should take place.

After I provided my students with this workable model, I allowed them access to information and resources and encouraged them to unpack the relationship between filmmaker and audience in a dynamic, rigorous way. I then allowed them to work at their own pace with regularly scheduled consultations. I found that the students were so genuinely engaged with the work they were doing, and so interested in producing a seminar that was nuanced and mature, that for the most part I could just leave them alone. I offered time where they could meet with me individually during a lesson to unpack certain aspects or check their analyses. As I'd not seen all of their film selections (we had a wide range and some titles were quite obscure), there was no risk of them merely parroting back information I'd already told them.

The element of this stage that we seemed to keep coming back to was the idea of the filmmaker constructing their invited reading through selection and manipulation of particular film techniques. Fourteen-year-olds looked for meaning and intention in the most minute of details – a slightly wider field of focus

directly to the camera and YouTube and Vine stars who can make quick but lasting connections with their audiences. They saw the poignancy in archival footage of the mistreatment of animals balanced with sombre music and the maudlin, dulcet tones of the narrator. They questioned the effectiveness of text on screen and saw the way that it could, at times, alienate rather than speak to a desired audience.

They did it.

These girls, fourteen and fifteen years old, explored the very grown-up world of the documentary with a delicacy and a nuance that people twice their age would have been proud of. Providing them with a framework underpinned by high expectations and equipping them with the appropriate analytical tools gave them the confidence to approach, unpack and attack content that they may have previously dismissed as being too advanced for them. The documentary was not something that they suffered through with drooping eyelids before they were finally dismissed to go to lunch. It wasn't something thrown on by the supervising teacher who gave them a dull worksheet about characters and plot to scribble answers in while they texted under the table. The documentary was now an artform that they could feel confident about embracing, challenging and probing.

Look at the world that our students are going to be left with because of the decisions that we, the adults who supposedly know better, are making now. Arming teenagers with the kind of critical literacy and complex thinking via a task like this was an absolute privilege. Of all the film genres and forms, it could be argued that the documentary contains the most capacity for influencing change and ringing true to the lived experience of students immersed in a digital age. The documentary was created to protest, to inform, to educate, to enrage and to inspire.

O Captain! My Captain!

Louise Lavery is a freelance writer based in Brisbane. She worked as a senior English teacher for over ten years in schools across Queensland and Victoria. **SE**

Endnotes

1. See Naima Karp, 'Why I Hate That I'm Part of the Snapchat Generation', *Pucker Mob*, 2015, <http://www.puckermob.com/lifestyle/why-i-hate-that-im-part-of-the-snapchat-generation>; Tracy McVeigh, 'How Big-hearted Babies Turn into Selfish Monsters', *The Guardian*, 4 May 2014, <https://www.theguardian.com/lifeandstyle/2014/may/04/how-babies-turn-into-selfish-monsters>; and Catherine Pearson, 'Teenagers' Values: More Materialistic, Less Interested in Work than Ever', *The Huffington Post*, 5 February 2013, <http://www.huffingtonpost.com.au/entry/teenagers-values-materialistic-work_n_3193782>, all accessed 29 March 2017.
2. See 'Kylie Jenner Talks About Her Insecurities, Admits She's Afraid of Negative Press Despite Immense Success', *Realty Today*, 2 December 2015, <http://www.realtytoday.com/articles/57930/20151202/kylie-jenner-talks-insecurities-admits-s-afraid-negative-press-despite.htm>, accessed 29 March 2017.
3. See <https://www.shortoftheweek.com/channels/documentary>, accessed 22 March 2017.

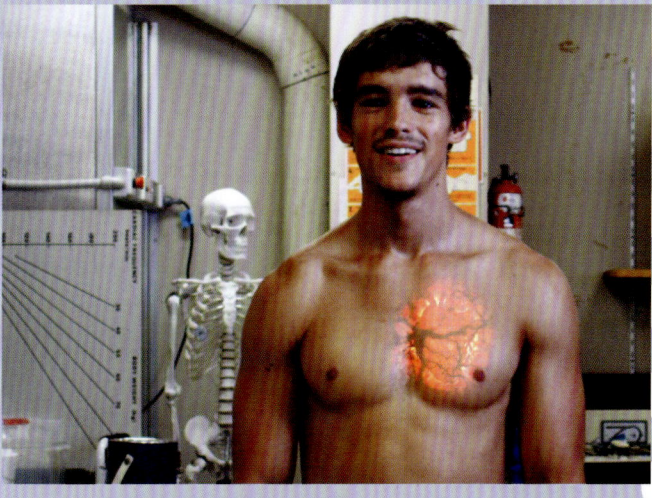

FROM TOP: *Super Size Me* (two images); *That Sugar Film* (two images)

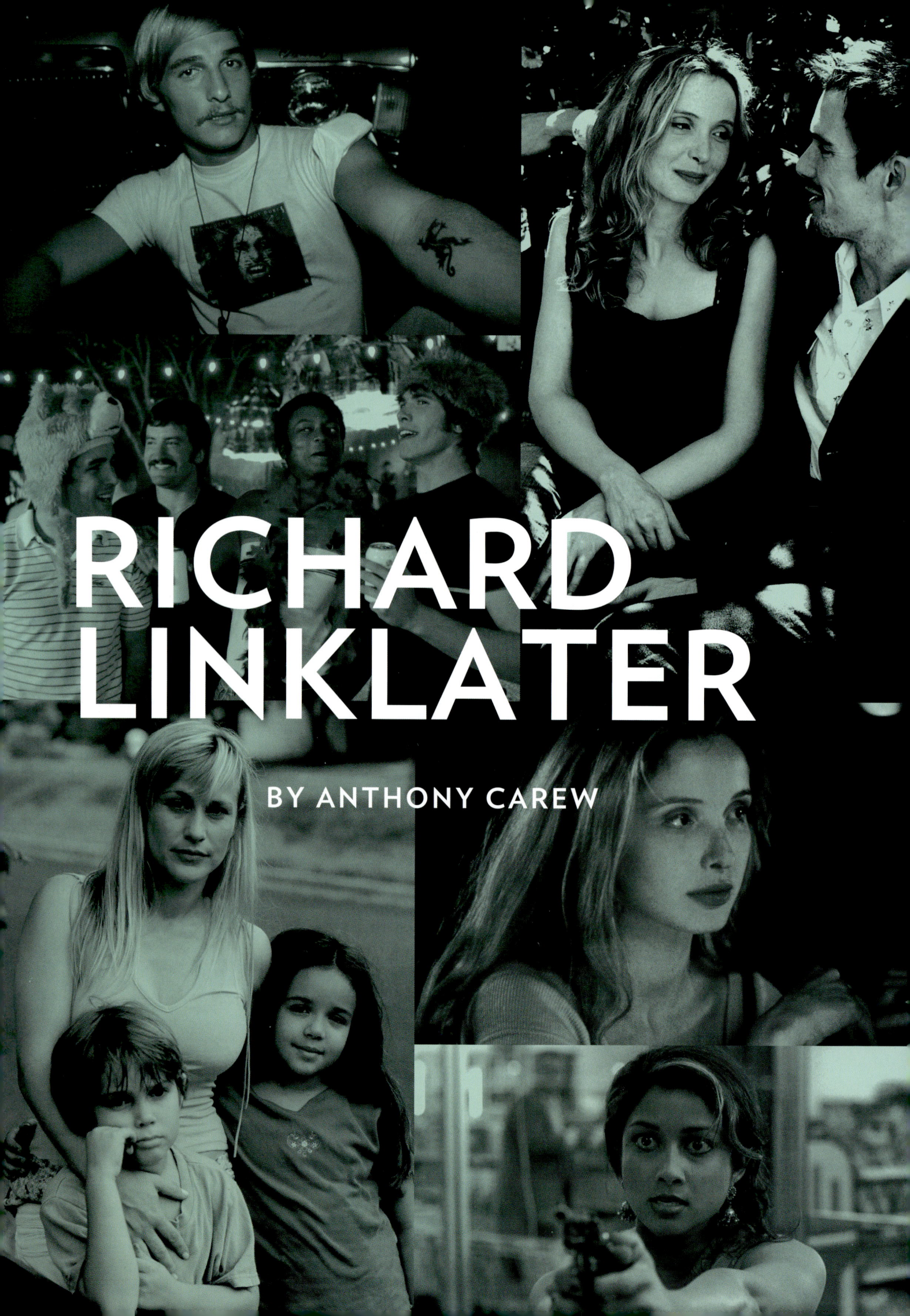

In Richard Linklater's timeless screen romance *Before Sunrise* (1995), its central paramours – having alighted from a train in Vienna, walking through the city discussing life and the universe – talk about the concept of documentaries that observe human beings going through their quotidian routines. Céline (Julie Delpy) wonders why anyone would be interested in 'all those mundane, boring things everybody has to do every day of their fucking life'. Jesse (Ethan Hawke), however, calls it 'the poetry of day-to-day life'.

The poetry of day-to-day life is Linklater's cinematic metier. Though singular works have explored genre or toured off in experimental directions, his filmography is filled with stories that are simple, relatable, human – free from contrived conflicts, genre tropes and violence. 'I think I have a low threshold of what a movie can be,' Linklater says. 'I'm kind of a minimalist. I'm like, "Can a movie be about something so simple?" [I'm trying] to find out if I can […] really go all the way with one idea.'[1]

And so, Linklater has made three films about one ongoing conversation (*Before Sunrise*; *Before Sunset*, 2004; and *Before Midnight*, 2013), three films about teenagers hanging out (*Dazed and Confused*, 1993; *SubUrbia*, 1996; *Everybody Wants Some!!*, 2016), and one film about an entire youth filled largely with conversations (*Boyhood*, 2014). His breakout second movie, *Slacker* (1991) – made when he was just thirty – is a series of loosely connected monologues, flowing from one philosophical discussion (or rant) to the next, an approach he revisited with the groundbreaking animation *Waking Life* (2001), a film based on his experiences with lucid dreaming.

Linklater was born in Houston, Texas, in 1960, and bounced around Texas, often trailing after his divorced mother, with his formative adolescent years spent in the '*Last Picture Show*–type town'[2] of Huntsville, Texas. Linklater loved both literature and baseball, winning a Scholastic Art and Writing award, as well as earning a baseball scholarship to Sam Houston State University. In his sophomore year, however, he was diagnosed with the heart condition atrial fibrillation, and his sporting career was instantly over. Laid up, with time on his hands, Linklater began obsessively reading and writing, turning his focus to theatre studies. But, soon after, he dropped out, and went to work on an offshore oil rig in the Gulf of Mexico. There, he spent all his downtime reading, and saved up money to buy a super 8 camera and some film stock.

Moving to Austin, Linklater set about building a community, founding the Austin Film Society, and creating a small-town network of students, oddballs and free spirits who could work on his films. His first feature, *It's Impossible to Learn to Plow by Reading Books* (1988), was entirely self-financed and self-made; Linklater served as its writer, director, star, cinematographer and editor, cutting the film at night at a local public-access TV station. Though it never received any distribution, it allowed Linklater to cut his teeth, and emboldened the filmmaker with a strong DIY streak. His second film, *Slacker*, was again self-financed, and shot with friends around his neighbourhood in Austin. But this film found critical acclaim while also having a surprising impact – its colloquial title pushed the slang term 'slacker' into the mainstream – and is considered a landmark in the American independent cinema movement.

From there, Linklater has become one of the most productive directors in American cinema, having made eighteen narrative features (and counting: 2017 will find the release of *Last Flag Flying* and the filming of *Where'd You Go, Bernadette*). Linklater is forever writing, and always at work; the filmmaker is so prolific that, at one point, *A Scanner Darkly* (2006), *Bad News Bears* (2005) and *Boyhood* were all simultaneously in production. Linklater's restlessness has meant that he's toured through genres, from western (*The Newton Boys*, 1998), kids movie (*School of Rock*, 2003) and issues film (*Fast Food Nation*, 2006) to period piece (*Me and Orson Welles*, 2008) and true crime (*Bernie*, 2011). He's occasionally intersected with the studio system, but has never become part of the Hollywood machine, maintaining his independence, and returning, after his various wanderings, to his particularly personal form of cinema. Linklater will forever be best known – especially after the Oscar-winning success of *Boyhood* – as a director dealing with time on screen, both within the texts of his films, and in the way the *Before* series and *Boyhood* play out over years, the actors actually ageing before our very eyes.

FILMS

Slacker

Linklater's breakout second feature was a 'summer art project',[3] a collective endeavour that was first sketched out in a twenty-four-hour period, shot in his Austin neighbourhood, made for US$23,000 on maxed-out credit cards, and filmed by a crew of friends who were all deferring payment for their services. Like Linklater's most famous films, it was born from a simple idea, which he'd dreamt up, years before, when the notion of a film career was itself a dream. 'It was one of those early radical ideas you have,' Linklater says, 'when you're trying to break out of everything that's come before […] I kinda saw the move as maybe fifty movies going on simultaneously, and you're just jumping from one to the next'.[4]

In a formalist gambit that Linklater makes fun, lively and seemingly spontaneous, *Slacker* is a non-narrative feature, its 'story' passed from one character to another, all of whom rant away in oft-sarcastic soliloquys. 'Dialogue as a kind of monologue in which the interior is brought forth,' Linklater wrote in the pro-

> In a formalist gambit that Linklater makes fun, lively and seemingly spontaneous, *Slacker* is a non-narrative feature, its 'story' passed from one character to another, all of whom rant away in oft-sarcastic soliloquys.

duction notes handed out to cast and crew. 'Actors speaking as if to themselves, in alternating monologues, self-analysis …'[5]

The cast – of over 100 characters – is filled largely with non-professionals, from Linklater himself to various local oddballs, musicians and personalities. The characters in the film are a collection of his people, from his town: dropouts, burnouts, beatniks, anarchists, conspiracy theorists, barstool philosophers, jaded intellectuals – lost and directionless daydreamers to whom 1980s America has offered very little. This theme struck a chord with youthful audiences: first earning a cult local following at its earliest screenings in Austin, *Slacker* eventually made US$1.2 million at the US box office. By making films entirely on his own, Linklater had put himself on the map, and shown the powers that be that he was the best kind of filmmaker: a profitable one.

Dazed and Confused, SubUrbia and Everybody Wants Some!!

After *Slacker*, Linklater graduated to making a studio film, pitching the idea of a rock'n'roll teen comedy to Universal; producer Jim Jacks sold the studio on the idea that *Dazed and Confused* could be a modern *American Graffiti* (George Lucas, 1973). Except, in hindsight, Linklater feels as if he put one over on the studio system,[6] getting US$6 million to make a personal, autobiographical, very Linklateresque film. He initially had the idea to make a film set inside one car in one night, inspired by his memories of idle adolescent nights, killing time. He conceived of it as an anti-eighties teen movie: 'At that time, teen movies were John Hughes movies,' Linklater said. 'There was so much drama. Maybe I'm an undramatic guy, but I remember a complete lack of anything big going on in high-school.'[7]

And so, *Dazed and Confused* is another teeming ensemble film (seventy-eight characters!), in which the last day of school in 1976 in suburban Austin involves initiation rites for incoming high school freshmen, a lot of philosophical conversations and, eventually, a big party. There's a fistfight, flirtations and first kisses, but the dramatic stakes are low, and the film's permissive portrayal of drug culture was hardly what a studio was hoping for merely a year after Bill Clinton was forced to deny he ever inhaled. In hindsight, though, *Dazed and Confused* may be the definitive teen film: a time capsule that feels timeless, its characters grappling with the passing of time, small-town mentalities and adolescent oppression, yet unsure if the looming adult world will offer them any respite, any reward. And its cast – members of which were, at the time, all unknowns – is filled with future stars: Ben Affleck, Milla Jovovich, Adam Goldberg, Rory Cochrane, Parker

> In hindsight, *Dazed and Confused* may be the definitive teen film: a time capsule that feels timeless, its characters grappling with the passing of time, small-town mentalities and adolescent oppression, yet unsure if the looming adult world will offer them any respite, any reward.

Posey, Nicky Katt, Renée Zellweger and, most famously, Matthew McConaughey, who steals the show in his very first film performance as the endlessly quotable lothario Wooderson.

Linklater followed *Dazed and Confused* with another teen film, *SubUrbia*, with which it shares some similarities (and actors), but a distinctly different spirit. Again, he's depicting the tedium of life in suburban Texas: disaffected youths bouncing between their parents' houses, parking lots and pool halls. But, this time, the director's working from a script by the more caustic Eric Bogosian, in which youthful aimlessness has curdled into cruel hostility, its characters petty, jealous, aggressive, petulant, bigoted. 'I'm an American. I was born here. I'm owed something,' barks Katt's discharged military vet, his resentment at the desi proprietors of the local convenience store symbolising white male entitlement and all-American racism, displaying the kind of darkness rarely seen

THIS PAGE: *Dazed and Confused* (three images)

THIS PAGE, FROM TOP: *Dazed and Confused*; *Everybody Wants Some!!*

in Linklater's filmography. Where *Dazed and Confused* remains perennial, *SubUrbia* feels all too nineties: full of self-loathing, surrender and concerns about 'selling out', all coming wrapped in a marketable grunge-rock package (a score by Sonic Youth!). For those listening closely, though, *SubUrbia*, like *Dazed and Confused*, houses a conversational reference to *Gilligan's Island*, as does Linklater's return to the idleness of gangs of youths, *Everybody Wants Some!!*

Almost a quarter-century after *Dazed and Confused*, Linklater would make the 'spiritual sequel' he'd long been hoping to. Another autobiographical period piece in which the ensemble cast ripples with both bonhomie and ennui, *Everybody Wants Some!!* is set in 1980, in the first few days of college, before classes have started (a liminal time that was also where his previous film, *Boyhood*, left off). Blake Jenner stars as the essential Linklater stand-in, a freshman arriving at school on a baseball scholarship

Everybody Wants Some!! soon moves beyond pissing contests and skirt-chasing: it weighs up the fluid personal identities of the college years; philosophises on what awaits once playing days have passed; and, eventually, miraculously summons a sweet, real-feeling romance.

at a fictional Texas university. On showing up, he's thrown into a house full of his fellow baseballers – a crew of oddballs, macho peacocks and jock philosophers; the ensemble, as with *Dazed and Confused*, is full of memorable characters ('I was in awe of how Linklater is able to bring so many fully realized characters to life in such a short time,' said filmmaker Hannah Fidell,[8] of *Everybody Wants Some!!*). Again, there's no real story; there's more the sense of hanging out, for a weekend, with the guys on the team. At first blush, it's a film about hyper-competitive men turning everything into a contest, and the rituals of initiation, ball-busting and male bonding in the group dynamic. But, Linklater being Linklater, *Everybody Wants Some!!* soon moves beyond pissing contests and skirt-chasing: it weighs up the fluid personal identities of the college years; philosophises on what awaits once playing days have passed; and, eventually, miraculously summons a sweet, real-feeling romance between Jake (Jenner) and Zoey Deutch's performing-arts student Beverly, a female foil who's allowed intellect, independence and agency of her own.

THIS PAGE, CLOCKWISE FROM TOP LEFT: *SubUrbia* (two images); *Everybody Wants Some!!* (two images); *SubUrbia* (two images); *Everybody Wants Some!!*

The *Before* films

Linklater's most famous film series is an ongoing romance, spanning three movies made across eighteen years. After working with big ensembles with *Slacker* and *Dazed and Confused*, for his fourth feature, *Before Sunrise*, Linklater wanted to do something different, stripping the film down to two actors and a small crew. The result is one of cinema's greatest boy-meets-girl stories, in which a pair of twentysomethings – an American, Jesse, and a Frenchwoman, Céline – spontaneously spend a night walking around Vienna, talking, drawing closer to each other. It has the stripped-down simplicity of Éric Rohmer's New Wave films, but with a warmth, humanity and sense of conversational joy that is distinctly Linklater's. To make sure the story was equally balanced between the male and female perspectives, Linklater co-wrote the script with his friend Kim Krizan, who'd appeared in *Slacker* and *Dazed and Confused* but had never written a screenplay; and, then, once he'd found his two actors, he rehearsed, revised and re-interpreted the heady, philosophical conversations that had been scripted. Making *Before Sunrise*, Linklater was out to capture that moment of first meeting: the electric feeling of connection, the crackling air of sexual attraction, how every instant is pregnant with possibility. It's also about how fleeting, ephemeral experiences can linger much more than fully experienced relationships, playing up to that romantic notion by posing a finale where the two characters part without exchanging contact information, pledging to meet six months later.

> Making *Before Sunrise*, Linklater was out to capture that moment of first meeting: the electric feeling of connection, the crackling air of sexual attraction, how every instant is pregnant with possibility.

THIS PAGE: *Before Sunrise*

The ambiguous, open-ended conclusion to *Before Sunrise* leaves off perfectly, but it also served, in the years following the film, as a litmus test for one's own sense of romance. When Linklater, Hawke and Delpy decided to revisit the story nine years later, Linklater throws that question – 'Do they end up together?' – back at audiences in cute, self-referential fashion. *Before Sunset* opens, nine years later, with Jesse now a novelist, on a book tour in Paris, answering questions from journalists who ask him – as they'd done of Linklater following his film's release – just that. Jesse has written a fictional account of the couple's original night together, and at a reading he sees that Céline has unexpectedly shown up, as if rematerialising from the past, a memory come back to life. After the reading is over, they begin talking, and with an hour to kill before Jesse needs to leave for the airport, they get reacquainted. And so, in real time, the conversation picks up where it left off; moonlit Vienna is exchanged for sun-dappled Paris, another European city serving as backdrop for a cinematic conversation piece. But, where *Before Sunrise* was rooted in a kind of collegiate malaise – young people filled with both dreams and uncertainty – *Before Sunset* finds the characters in their thirties, the abrupt rupture of seeing each other again stirring up not just their old feelings for each other, but old feelings of their youth. Each has settled, but is unhappy, restless; Jesse is now a young father (as Hawke himself was, at the time), and Céline has not found the satisfaction in relationships that she has in her career as environmental advocate. The film, again, concludes with an open-ended finale, in which the pair return to Céline's apartment, and she warns him, finally, 'you are gonna miss that plane'.

After leaving the 'Do they end up together?' question lingering a second time, Linklater is, initially, in no hurry to answer it at the beginning of the third film in the series, *Before Midnight*. The film opens with Jesse at the airport with his son, Hank (Seamus Davey-Fitzpatrick), being put on a plane back home after spending a summer together in Greece. When Jesse returns to his car, we discover he and Céline have twin girls (as Linklater does in real life), and have been together since their reconnection in Paris. Of course, picking up with our familiar couple nine years on does anything but stir up the old romance. Linklater has always thought of his series as 'romance for realists',[9] and *Before Midnight* is where the realism comes in, exchanging Rohmeresque sweetness for a bitter portrait of marriage more indebted to Ingmar Bergman. The pair have spent a summer, with the three kids, at a picturesque house in the Peloponnese, surrounded by various other intellectuals and locals. It's been a beautiful respite, but with their trip coming to an end, issues from their lives back home are starting to creep in: Céline, tired of working in the non-profit sector, is considering a job within the French government; Jesse, tired of the distance between him, in Paris, and his son, in Chicago, yearns to return to America. Their friends in Greece have paid for a night in a hotel and organised care of the twins, leaving Céline and Jesse to spend a supposed 'romantic' evening together. Only, contrivance has nothing on spontaneity, and, left alone together, the two end up fighting, the ongoing conversation becoming a long argument staged with lacerating barbs and caustic sarcasm, Linklater never looking away, or alleviating the tension. It's a far cry from the sweetness of the first two films, but just as honest.

Taken as a trio of works ('trilogy' feels like the wrong term), the *Before* series is a remarkable depiction of how people, and relationships, change over time – of what brings them together, what keeps them together and what drives them apart. *Before Sunrise* and *Before Sunset* are beloved for their romantic depiction of conversational sparring and human connection, but *Before Midnight* feels just as meaningful, showing the sadder, harsher, more combative realities that inevitably arrive in any relationship.

THIS PAGE, FROM TOP: *Before Midnight*; *Before Sunset* (two images)

Waking Life and A Scanner Darkly

After his first real failure as director – the big-budget western *The Newton Boys*, which was a box office flop – Linklater returned to Austin. His seventh feature, *Waking Life*, is a collaboration with animator Bob Sabiston, who created a rotoscoping computer program that allows artists to animate directly over digital video footage. The result is a film that looks like nothing that'd come before, its animation style switching as a result of each of the thirty-one animators working on different sections, the ever-changing line and erratic rendering creating a fluid, liquid quality. But, while he blazed a new technological trail, Linklater was really returning to his roots. *Waking Life* is essentially 'Slacker: The Cartoon', an animated film in which verbose vignettes are strung together. It features characters from *Slacker* and *Before Sunrise*, on-screen turns by Linklater and Krizan, and the first screen appearance of Linklater's daughter, Lorelei, who'd go on to star in *Boyhood*.

Waking Life is essentially 'Slacker: The Cartoon', an animated film in which verbose vignettes are strung together.

Inspired by Linklater's own experience with lucid dreaming, it's a cinematic attempt to enter the dream space: surreal, delirious, odd. 'Some of it was kind of absurdist, like from a strange movie,' says the film's unnamed protagonist (*Dazed and Confused*'s Wiley Wiggins), describing his dream within the film's dream. This prospect is later mocked by Steven Soderbergh, who recounts a story about Billy Wilder and Louis Malle, whose essential moral is that any 'dream within a dream' film is a sure financial failure. As its protagonist wanders through his dreams, he hears people – many of them professors – talking on existentialism, postmodernism, linguistics, evolution, physics and free will, philosophy, cinema, self-awareness and, of course, dreams. 'I don't consider the film experimental,' Linklater said. 'I'm just trying to replicate the mind'.[10]

THIS PAGE: *Waking Life*

Waking Life ends with Linklater himself talking about Philip K Dick writing *Flow My Tears, the Policeman Said*. And the director would return to rotoscoping to adapt a different Dick book, *A Scanner Darkly*. Befitting its author, it's a story of paranoia, though Linklater's particular cinematic approach doesn't allow it to ever, really, become a paranoia-thriller. It's set in a near-future surveillance-state California, where a drug epidemic has swept through Los Angeles – 20 per cent of the population is addicted to a drug called Substance D – and detectives listen in on suspected users. Dick wrote his original book based on his experiences hanging out with drug addicts, out to depict the dark fallout from the doped-out end of the 1960s. As its small-time drug users hole up in a sharehouse, growing obsessed with the feeling that they're being watched, it becomes clear that the story is also about minds split in two and people living double lives; ultimately, *A Scanner Darkly* is also a condemnation of the dual all-American industries of drugs and the war on drugs.

> Ultimately, *A Scanner Darkly* is a condemnation of the dual all-American industries of drugs and the war on drugs.

Linklater shot *A Scanner Darkly* in just six weeks, with the film's starry cast – Keanu Reeves, an excellently twitchy Robert Downey Jr, Woody Harrelson, Winona Ryder – all working for scale pay to keep the budget down. But the laborious, ultimately troubled process of animating the video footage dragged on for years ('[people] think it's a filter and that it's done by a computer,' Sabiston said. 'It's not at all, though. It's hand-drawn'[11]), Linklater describing the animation process, when compared to *Waking Life*, as 'more of a factory and less artists expressing themselves'.[12] Despite the fact that Linklater talks about *A Scanner Darkly*, in hindsight, as somewhat of a disappointment, the film does leave us with one indelible, singular image: a 'scramble suit' – a form of camouflage for its wearer that projects a facade of ever-shifting visages, a surreal facial kaleidoscope that ably achieves the film's intended hallucinogenic effect.

THIS PAGE: *A Scanner Darkly*

Boyhood

Linklater had long wanted to make a film about childhood, but could never work out what moment he wanted to chronicle. Then, inspiration struck: 'it hit me that I could just depict a life over numerous years and make it a much longer-term project with the prospect of the people getting older'.[13] And so, Linklater came up with a concept: he'd shoot a twelve-minute film once a year for twelve years, with his leading actor growing from a child to an adult as he did. 'It's a little bit like timelapse photography of a human being,' said Hawke.[14] 'Everybody kind of wonders, how do you change over time?' said the film's star, Ellar Coltrane. '[T]o see all of these different versions of myself just catalogued together … it's incredible. Very surreal.'[15]

It's a simple idea that only someone as self-contained, driven and disciplined as Linklater could bring to screen, *Boyhood* a production miracle unrivalled in cinema history. 'We started this film 4,207 days ago,' Linklater said upon its premiere. 'We think that's the longest production in history […] But it was only 39 official days of shooting over that twelve-year period, usually about three days a year with a few extra days here and there.'[16]

The resulting film lives out Linklater's dream: Mason (Coltrane), going from six years old to eighteen in front of his camera – from innocent kid to a garrulous, philosophical, Linklateresque figure in 160 minutes. Each year is a time capsule, not just of its cast, but of technology (each chapter

bringing a different mobile phone), and music (its through-the-years soundtrack including Coldplay, Sheryl Crow, Phoenix, Gotye). Aside from a terrible drunken-stepdad storyline, there's little blown-out drama in *Boyhood*; instead, it's a film about the long process of growing up, the slow sense of self-discovery, and burgeoning identity. But, in a grander sense, it's about how kids get dragged through the lives of their parents, and how parents – especially when separated – have to balance living their own lives versus being concerned with their kids' lives. Patricia Arquette won an Oscar for Best Supporting Actress as Mason's

> It's a simple idea that only someone as self-contained, driven and disciplined as Linklater could bring to screen, *Boyhood* a production miracle unrivalled in cinema history.

mother, while Hawke scored a nomination for Best Supporting Actor as his largely absent father. *Boyhood* received six Oscar nominations in total, including for Best Director and Best Picture, and may be the most acclaimed Linklater film in a career full of acclaimed films.

DISTINGUISHING FEATURES

Philosophical conversations

In Linklater's films, seemingly everyone – jocks, stoners, slackers, professors, publishers, drunks, druggies, conspiracy theorists, tourists, workers, preachers – is up for long, sometimes discursive discussions re: life, love, humanity, society, temporality, religion, reincarnation, reality, romance, media and corporate interests. This, of course, comes from Linklater himself: the filmmaker is a voracious reader, deep thinker and rambling raconteur. His scripts are duly wordy, but over periods of rehearsal, he works with actors to make sure his conversations feel conversational, that their wordiness scans as realist. 'I always say the director in me fires the writer before we even start shooting. It's just whatever makes it seem real,' Linklater has said.[17]

Sometimes – as in moments of *Slacker*, *Dazed and Confused*, *Boyhood* and *Everybody Wants Some!!* – those conversations take in popular culture, discussing male fantasy in *Gilligan's Island*, the respective musical qualities of Pink Floyd and Van Halen, and even, with amusing foreshadowing, the unlikely event of there ever being more *Star Wars* films. Other times, as with much of *Waking Life* and the *Before* series, Linklater is reaching for the truly big questions, trying to understand the experience of existence; he uses cinema – the artform most evocative of dreams and memories – to address the passage of time.

Time

'When I think about storytelling, it always comes back to time,' says Linklater.[18] Time is what a director is 'manipulating, recording, capturing', but it's also the most universal human experience, the grist of existence. And Linklater, as philosophical thinker, is always drawn to time.

A Scanner Darkly

'Time is an illusion,' Linklater himself says, on screen – albeit under layers of animation – at the culmination of *Waking Life*. It's a film about perception and reality, and his character, in the middle of a cinematic dream within a dream, is recounting a dream of his own, in which Lady Gregory has said, in a meaning-of-life kind of way, 'there's only one instant, and it's right now, and it's eternity'. In the narrative skips of *Waking Life* and *Slacker*, Linklater is turning the 'parallel universes' theory into cinema, and these theories of existence come up even in conversation between lovers in the *Before* series.

'Think of this as time travel,' Jesse says to Céline when trying to convince her to get off the train at the start of *Before Sunrise*, talking up this opportunity as a way of making sure he wouldn't come to be some if-only one-who-got-away, and that it's a 'favour' to her future self, and future husband. This hypothetical scenario actually comes to bear at the end of *Before Midnight*, when Jesse himself has become her sad husband; in the face of this, he turns, again, to the notion of time travel, claiming to be a traveller bringing a message to Céline from her future self. In *Before Sunset*, the novel Jesse's written about their first meeting is called 'This Time'; the song at the end, that Céline dances to, is 'Just in Time'; Linklater considers the films to be about 'romance and time'.[19]

Linklater shows his obsession with time in the way he structures his stories, often setting them in specific windows of time. *Slacker*, *Dazed and Confused*, *SubUrbia*, the rape-revenge camcorder flick *Tape* (2001), and the three *Before* films all take place in a day, while *Before Sunset* takes place in something close to real time. *Everybody Wants Some!!* lasts one weekend, and *Waking Life* spans the space of a dream. *Boyhood* is, with its twelve-year production, at the opposite end, but when it was being edited Linklater thought of titling the film – drawn from a line in its final scene – 'Always Now', which suggested, he thought, the way *Boyhood* forever beats on into the present.

Time also becomes an active element in the way his movies have persisted long past their initial releases, remaining in the popular consciousness and changing as days go by. Linklater's best films haven't been forgotten, but remain perennial; the cult followings of *Dazed and Confused* and *Before Sunrise* allowed the filmmaker to return to them, years later, to make sequels both spiritual and literal.

Texas

Ten of Linklater's eighteen narrative features have been set in Texas, and another, *A Scanner Darkly*, was shot in Austin, even though it is set in Anaheim, California. When Hollywood was calling early in his career, Linklater made a deliberate decision to just 'do his own thing' in Austin, setting up a production

> Both *Dazed* and its spiritual sequel feature characters that could be called 'intellectualist jocks'; this, essentially, is where the equally bookish and brawny Linklater sat in the teenage social spectrum.

Richard Linklater on the set of *Before Sunrise*

company, and helping build a local film community. 'I feel lucky to have been able to stay here and make movies, because I always want to depict that other part of Texas,' says Linklater.[20] Texas isn't a mere backdrop, but a part of his stories: *The Newton Boys* and *Bernie* are both based on local incidents of crime; the latter, Linklater has said, is filled with people who could be his mother's friends. *Boyhood*'s childhood-spanning tale is universal, but it's filled with specifically Texan details: a classroom saying the Texas pledge at the start of a school day; Hawke's deadbeat dad taking his kids to see the Houston Astros play; Mason receiving a bible and a shotgun from his step-grandparents as a fifteenth birthday gift.

Autobiography

From the moment he put himself in his first film, *It's Impossible to Learn to Plow by Reading Books*, Linklater has been making a particularly personal kind of cinema. His second film, *Slacker*, opens with him on screen, and then moves through a cast of characters inhabiting the Austin neighbourhood in which he was living. *Dazed and Confused* – from its drives in circles to its adult-condoned hazing rituals to the surnames of many of its characters – draws directly from his youth; *Everybody Wants Some!!*, from his experiences of attending college on a baseball scholarship. Both *Dazed* and its spiritual sequel feature characters that could be called 'intellectualist jocks'; this, essentially, is where the equally bookish and brawny Linklater sat in the teenage social spectrum.

Before Sunrise was inspired by an experience from Linklater's own life. In 1989, just after he'd finished shooting *Slacker*, he was in Philadelphia, staying with his sister, when he met a woman, Amy Lehrhaupt, by chance.[21] The two spent a night, from midnight to 6am, walking and talking; and, even as it was happening, Linklater was thinking cinematically: 'This could be a movie,' he marvelled. 'If I could just capture this feeling I'm having right now'.[22]

And *Boyhood* drew heavily on Linklater's own childhood. Like Arquette's character in the film, his mother was a divorcee who went back to school, leading Linklater from town to town, and boyfriend to boyfriend. 'My mom's a pretty strong woman, but you might question her judgment,' Linklater has said[23] of her romantic choices; the men of *Boyhood* are called, by its protagonist, 'a parade of drunken assholes'. Because of how much it drew from their lives, he worried about showing the film to his mother,[24] but for Linklater, mining the personal has long been his working way.

Young people

'Teenagers [are] trapped wherever their parents live,' says Linklater. 'Teenagers have always been miserable and oppressed. Their parents oppress them, their schools oppress them, their local environment oppresses. There's no place to go.'[25]

In *Dazed and Confused*, *SubUrbia* and *Boyhood*, Linklater has made some of cinema's most truthful portraits of teenage years, about idle times spent hanging in parking lots, the search for identity, and the percolating rebellion that has kids wanting to challenge the institutions of family, school, church and state. Even when his characters graduate to college – in *Everybody Wants Some!!*, *Before Sunrise* or, eventually, in *Boyhood* – they struggle with who they are, what they're doing and what their lives mean. 'College is about figuring out what to do with all the adult freedom that's suddenly been dropped in your lap,' Linklater says.[26]

THIS PAGE, FROM TOP: *Before Midnight*; Linklater on the set of *Boyhood*

Towards the end of *Boyhood*, its protagonist has finally graduated from high school, and he heads off for a night at a bar with his dad. While Mason Sr is counselling Mason Jr on romantic travails, he imparts greater wisdom about the passing of time. 'You get older, you don't feel as much. Your skin gets tougher,' he says; the raw, vivid, overwhelming feelings of youth are something that, as you get older, 'you've gotta hold onto'.

'I'm interested in identity and people who're still figuring out who they are,' Linklater says. 'I still feel that myself, even if I've got 20 years' distance on what I'm depicting [so] that will always slant me toward younger people.'27

https://clickv.ie/w/screen-ed/boyhood

Anthony Carew is a Melbourne-based critic. **SE**

Endnotes

1. Richard Linklater, quoted in Jacob Stolworthy, 'Richard Linklater Interview: "*Everybody Wants Some* Is a Continuation of *Boyhood*"', *The Independent*, 10 May 2016, <http://www.independent.co.uk/arts-entertainment/films/features/richard-linklater-everybody-wants-some-interview-boyhood-before-sunrise-a7020961.html>, accessed 21 April 2017.
2. Richard Linklater, in 'Richard Linklater on Making Independent Movies', YouTube, 14 December 2012, <https://www.youtube.com/watch?v=hLl468VZsYU>, accessed 21 April 2017.
3. Richard Linklater, in '*Slacker, Dazed and Confused, Before Sunrise*: Richard Linklater Interview, Filmmaking Education', YouTube, 25 June 2012, <https://www.youtube.com/watch?v=T6t_f_aWd_4>, accessed 21 April 2017.
4. ibid.
5. Richard Linklater, quoted in DVD booklet, *Slacker*, Criterion Collection, 2013.
6. See DVD booklet, *Dazed and Confused*, Criterion Collection, 2006.
7. ibid.
8. Hannah Fidell, quoted in Chris O'Falt, '35 Directors Pick Their Favorite Movies of 2016', *Indiewire*, 28 December 2016, <http://www.indiewire.com/2016/12/directors-2016-favorite-movies-tv-shows-jonathan-demme-paul-feig-marielle-heller-sam-esmail-david-lowery-jennifer-kent-1201763198/2/>, accessed 21 April 2017.
9. Ethan Hawke, quoted in Leslie Felperin, 'Don't Get Mad, Get Ethan', *The Age*, 1 August 2004, <http://www.theage.com.au/articles/2004/07/31/1091080450052.html>, accessed 9 April 2017.
10. Richard Linklater, quoted in Geoffrey Macnab, 'Richard Linklater: Life, Death, Love, Whatever', *The Independent*, 18 April 2002, <http://www.independent.co.uk/arts-entertainment/films/features/richard-linklater-life-death-love-whatever-9268959.html>, accessed 21 April 2017.

ABOVE, CLOCKWISE FROM LEFT: *Boyhood*; *Dazed and Confused*; *Everybody Wants Some!!*; *SubUrbia*; *Dazed and Confused* BELOW: Linklater on the set of *Waking Life*

[11] Bob Sabiston, quoted in Scott Tobias, '*A Scanner Darkly*'s Head of Animation Talks About the Film's Hellish Production', *The Dissolve*, 20 November 2014, <https://thedissolve.com/features/movie-of-the-week/827-a-scanner-darklys-head-of-animation-talks-about-th/>, accessed 21 April 2017.

[12] Richard Linklater, quoted in Robert La Franco, 'Trouble in Toowntown', *Wired*, 1 March 2006, <https://www.wired.com/2006/03/scanner-2/>, accessed 21 April 2017.

[13] Richard Linklater, quoted in Gavin Smith, 'Lost in America', *Film Comment*, July/August 2006, <https://www.filmcomment.com/article/lost-in-america-richard-linklater-interview/>, accessed 21 April 2017.

[14] Ethan Hawke, quoted in Kevin Jagernauth, 'Ethan Hawke Says Richard Linklater's Secret, Long Developing *Boyhood* Will Be Released in 2 Years', *Indiewire*, 6 June 2013, <http://www.indiewire.com/2013/06/ethan-hawke-says-richard-linklaters-secret-long-developing-boyhood-will-be-released-in-2-years-97239/>, accessed 21 April 2017.

[15] Ellar Coltrane, quoted in Emily Buder, '5 Things We Learned About Filmmaking from Richard Linklater's *Boyhood*', *Indiewire*, 23 June 2014, <http://www.indiewire.com/2014/06/5-things-we-learned-about-filmmaking-from-richard-linklaters-boyhood-25035/>, accessed 21 April 2017.

[16] Richard Linklater, quoted in Buder, ibid.

[17] Linklater, in '*Slacker, Dazed and Confused, Before Sunrise*', op. cit.

[18] Linklater, quoted in Buder, op. cit.

[19] Linklater, in '*Slacker, Dazed and Confused, Before Sunrise*', op. cit.

[20] ibid.

[21] Forrest Wickman, 'The Real Couple Behind *Before Sunrise*', *Slate*, 30 May 2013, <http://www.slate.com/blogs/browbeat/2013/05/30/before_sunrise_inspiration_before_midnight_is_dedicated_to_amy_lehrhaupt.html>, accessed 21 April 2017.

[22] Richard Linklater, quoted in Sarah Hepola, 'Summer Movies; Those Strangers on a Train, Nine Years Later', *The New York Times*, 9 May 2004, <http://www.nytimes.com/2004/05/09/movies/summer-movies-those-strangers-on-a-train-nine-years-later.html>, accessed 21 April 2017.

[23] Richard Linklater, quoted in Nicholas Dawidoff, 'Richard Linklater: About a *Boyhood*', *Rolling Stone*, 15 January 2015, <http://www.rollingstone.com/movies/features/richard-linklater-about-a-boyhood-20150115>, accessed 21 April 2017.

[24] Nathan Heller, 'Moment to Moment', *The New Yorker*, 30 June 2014, <http://www.newyorker.com/magazine/2014/06/30/moment-to-moment>, accessed 21 April 2017.

[25] Linklater, in '*Slacker, Dazed and Confused, Before Sunrise*', op. cit.

[26] Richard Linklater, quoted in Adam Nayman, '"I Have No Excuses": An Interview with Richard Linklater', *Hazlitt*, 20 April 2016, <http://hazlitt.net/feature/i-have-no-excuses-interview-richard-linklater>, accessed 21 April 2017.

[27] Linklater, quoted in Macnab, op. cit.

Marvel stories are big business. These modern myths are so ubiquitous across cinema, television, comic books, videogames and toys that every student would be familiar with at least part of the Marvel Universe. Beyond entertaining us with tales of superheroes, however, the construction of this universe can teach us much about what media convergence and transmedia storytelling look like in 2017, writes TYSON WILS.

Marvel filed for bankruptcy in 1996 due to 'a confluence of over-extended investments, costly development of films that were never produced, and a downturn in the comics industry'.[1] While one key factor for this downturn was a plunge in overall sales in comics in the second part of the 1990s, companies such as Marvel was also divested of their share of takings because of the rise of independent publishers who, since the 1980s, had been eating into Marvel's and DC's market shares of sales. Under the stewardship of figures such as Avi Arad, CEO of the company Toy Biz, which first became associated with Marvel in the early 1990s and then merged directly with it in 1998, a new 'programme of property licensing' began 'with the goal of re-balancing the Marvel ledgers'.[2]

At different stages in its history Marvel had licensed out characters before, allowing them to migrate to other media. This included television (see *The Marvel Super Heroes*, an animation series made in 1966; *The Incredible Hulk*, a live-action television series that ran for five seasons from 1977 to 1982; and *Captain America*, a made-for-television movie released in 1979 and directed by Rod Holcomb), films (*Return of Captain America*, a fifteen-part Saturday-afternoon serial film that first screened in 1944; *Howard the Duck*, William Huyck, 1986; *The Punisher*, Mark Goldblatt, 1989; and *Captain America*, Albert Pyun, 1990), and videogames (beginning with the Atari 2600 game *Spider-Man* in 1982). However, with a clear and hard-headed business approach, Arad and his associates wanted to steer Marvel properties into Hollywood; in particular, they wanted to build ongoing revenue out of Marvel's stock of characters by constructing a cinematic

PREVIOUS SPREAD: Iron Man in film form ABOVE: Early iterations of Marvel stories

universe of sequels, spin-offs and serial narratives. As part of, but also in addition to, this universe, they likewise wanted to develop tie-ins and storyworlds across various platforms – what can be referred to as transmedia storytelling. They wanted to create the kind of mass appeal that attracts both causal and niche audiences. To this end they franchised Marvel's characters, a strategy consistent with the entertainment approach that has been consolidated in Hollywood since at least the early 1990s (with prototypes of this strategy evident in various phases of the history of Hollywood blockbuster production). In sum, Arad and his team wanted to realise Marvel's potential to become an 'entertainment player of serious scale and complexity',[3] a potential Stan Lee, iconic figurehead of Marvel since the 1960s, had recognised early in his career and had been trying to make real since the late 1970s.

The first stage of this new approach to expanding the Marvel Universe ('Universe' in the sense here of Marvel comics, film, television and videogames that are under the intellectual property rights umbrella of Marvel) and brand by fully utilising the commercial potential of the company's properties involved licensing out its characters for a fee to studios such as 20th Century Fox (the *X-Men* trilogy, Bryan Singer, 2000 & 2003 and Brett Ratner, 2006; and the *Fantastic Four* movies, Tim Story, 2005 & 2007), and Sony and Columbia Pictures (the *Spider-Man* trilogy, Sam Raimi, 2002–2007). As Derek Johnson explains, 'license fees and royalties bolstered Marvel's revenues in time of need'[4] and 'provided an alternative revenue stream to support the company's tentative rebirth'.[5]

However, at this stage of Marvel's comeback, the company's control was essentially limited to pre-production. This is true even though, within a short space of time, it found it had the ability to help kickstart projects, and, by selling off rights to its characters to the motion-picture industry, it was helping to bolster the popularity of the superhero genre, which was in its interests to do since it was a way to promote its comic book titles. (It should be pointed out that such a market plan was by no means new to Marvel, since it had tied its comics to other media in the past, but it was a key part of its rebirth and a strategy it has continued to employ by trying to make the comics it has published as part of the Marvel Universe reboot – such as the *Secret Wars* series in 2015 – 'mirror the [Marvel Cinematic Universe] in order to bring in new readers and make the comics more commercially viable'.[6]) Nonetheless, studios like Sony-Columbia were making a lot of money on their *Spider-Man* pictures and Marvel was only receiving a small percentage of box office revenues. Put plainly: the company was not making enough money by simply licensing out its characters.

Moreover, as Johnson explains, 'this licensing model gave studios full control over development schedules – and thus control over how often Marvel could expect license royalties'.[7] This meant that Marvel had to operate with a level of unpredictability beyond the usual level of uncertainty that characterises the film industry. As is well known, it is hard, perhaps impossible, to ever guarantee that a film will be a hit, but not being able to control when films are released adds another level of difficulty for a company dependent on the ongoing production of films to create a stable revenue stream. Not to mention the fact that not having creative and economic control over production and distribution limited Marvel's capacity to guide the making of the films to which its name was attached to probable commercial success. It should also be remembered that for a company that found itself in the kind of financial slump Marvel did in the mid 1990s, and that wanted to realise its potential to be a major entertainment business strategically aligned with the Hollywood industry, control over being able to try to consistently produce blockbuster successes was very important. This is not simply because such successes would increase the amount of revenue the company would receive through fees and returns. It is also because predictable and healthy income is vital to investor interest and building corporate partnerships, both crucial if any thoughts about rapidly increasing the scope and scale of Marvel's role in moving its comic characters across to the medium of (Hollywood) film were going to be realised.

Regarding this latter point, it is worth noting that Marvel wanted to secure an industry position from where it could more effectively utilise the economic benefits of media convergence. It wanted to make sure that it could play a central role in fostering narrative expansion across various technologies and markets, extending

Marvel wanted to secure an industry position from where it could more effectively utilise the economic benefits of media convergence.

the characters and storylines developed in each film instalment to the content in tie-in videogames, animated productions and television shows. According to Johnson, the first kinds of licensing deals that were entered into were not conducive to Marvel achieving this goal:

Because Marvel depended on the mainstream visibility of [its] films to drive toys, video games, and other licensed markets, the health of those revenue streams required consistent, predictable film development. Furthermore, while one successful film could generate significant royalties for Marvel, licensing analysts insisted that film hits did not necessarily guarantee the success of related toys and video games, giving Marvel increased motivation to ensure that film development progressed in service of these other crucial licensed markets.[8]

THIS PAGE, CLOCKWISE FROM TOP: The X-Men; Spider-Man; an Incredible Hulk toy

Screen Education | No. 86

75

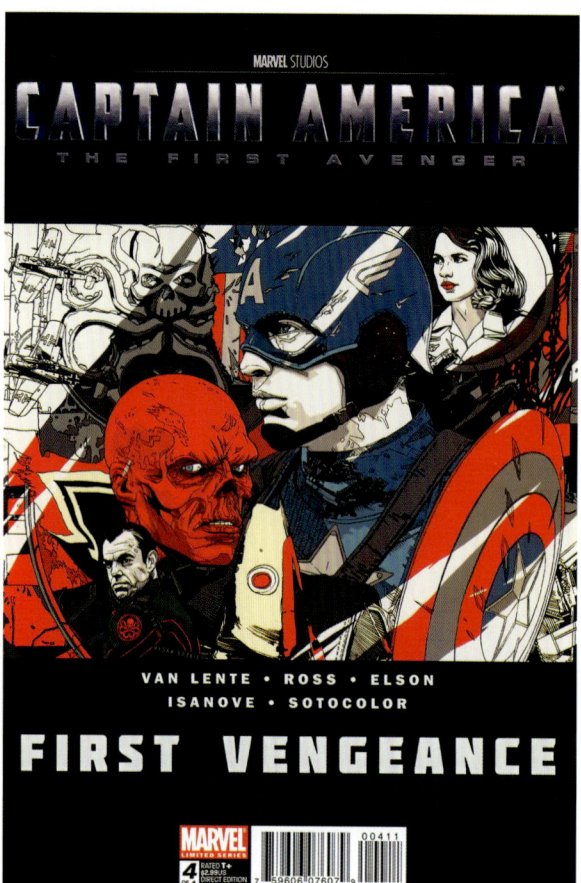

From the perspective of the studios, the licensing arrangements that Marvel entered into the late 1990s and early to mid 2000s provided the studios with direct access to material that had a built-in audience (including a relatively small, if nonetheless active and dedicated, comic book audience), a proven track record (not always a commercially successful record, but a record), and plotlines and character types that spanned across a long, deep history of storytelling that could be mined and recycled into the foreseeable future. In other words, it was a way for the majors to minimise risk by appropriating stories and characters that were still capable of succeeding – by investing 'only in those properties with proven market viability'.⁹

There are two key reasons why Marvel was able to regain creative and industrial control of its characters. First, because of the way it accrued and used capital from 2005 to 2008. The company used as collateral the money it had generated from licensing arrangements to build a line of credit with agencies outside of the Hollywood studio system, such as Merrill Lynch. Marvel struck a deal that 'provided budgets of between [US]$50 million and [US]$165 million per film, the profits from which could be reinvested'.¹⁰ While the deal was subject to an initial period of evaluation to ensure the 'proven viability of the investment',¹¹ and Marvel had to agree to hand over proprietary control of its characters if the first movies it made were not commercially successful, this still enabled the company to plan ahead for future film productions, something vital for Marvel because it wanted to weave a tapestry of interconnected films that were also projected to tie in with other media products. With this newfound cash flow, Marvel also hastily bought back rights to characters that it had previously sold off, such as Iron Man and the Hulk. This also helped the company to plan for a 'coordinated roll-out'¹² of films.

For instance, the first two *Iron Man* movies (Jon Favreau, 2008 & 2010), *The Incredible Hulk* (Louis Leterrier, 2008), *Thor* (Kenneth Branagh, 2011) and *Captain America: The First Avenger* (Joe Johnston, 2011) all contributed to a broader narrative that paved the way for the release of Joss Whedon's *The Avengers* in 2012. At the same time that future plot information was being seeded by each of these films, and, at least in the case of movies such as *Thor*, particular storylines were being developed that would be expanded in *The Avengers*, there were tie-ins with other media products, such as the comic books *Captain America: First Vengeance* (2011) and *The Avengers Prelude: Fury's Big Week* (2012).

Second, because of the kinds of partnerships Marvel entered into with the studios, beginning with the release of *Iron Man*, it was able to enter into distribution deals with the major studios – at first, Paramount (*Iron Man*) and Universal Studios (*The Incredible Hulk*). This allowed the company to retain the bulk of the profits made from its films due to low distribution fees, but also, perhaps more importantly, 'determine its own release schedules, and make further toy and video-game licensing deals without sharing revenue or authority with the studios'.¹³

While the popular and commercial success of *Iron Man* and *The Incredible Hulk* demonstrated to Wall Street backers like Merrill Lynch that doing business with Marvel was feasible, becoming a subsidiary of the Walt Disney Company in 2009 provided the company with the kind of financial backing it needed to take its business operations and, in turn, its relationship with Hollywood, to another level. From a purist point of view, Marvel could not call itself independent once it assimilated into Disney, a multinational, entertainment conglomerate. Nonetheless, being owned by Disney has meant greater and more diverse flows of capital, which, overall, has given Marvel more material and symbolic resources to use. For example, being part of Disney has opened up new global markets for the company to explore, and fostered new kinds of creative and strategic alliances.

Writing a year after the acquisition, Joseph Calandro reflected on how well Marvel's characters could be effectively 'aligned with Disney's extensive media and theme park platforms',[14] particularly given the latter's ability to leverage 'character content internationally'.[15] This has been evident, for instance, in the gradual bleed of 'Marvel characters into Disney-branded commercial and aesthetic space'.[16] Disney, for example, helped Marvel to adapt the Z-grade characters from *Guardians of the Galaxy*, 'who had almost no name recognition outside diehard comic fans',[17] and 'could not be found prominently in existing videogames, animated series, toys or miscellaneous merchandise',[18] into a film that had instant success at the box office. Part of the reason for this success was that Disney capitalised on the popularity of the Marvel brand and the then-recent success of films such as *The Avengers* to promote *Guardians of the Galaxy* (James Gunn, 2014) through a range of ancillary products prior to its release. Not only did Disney Consumer Products 'line up an array of licensees' in advance 'to produce toys and apparel around the film and its characters, especially Rocket Raccoon',[19] but it also promoted 'the availability of the *Guardians* characters for *Disney Infinity*' months before the film premiered.[20] Released in 2013 by Disney Interactive Studios, *Disney Infinity* is an action-adventure videogame with physical toys that is available for numerous gaming platforms. In terms of global sales, the game was performing very well by the middle of 2014,[21] which meant that Disney's marketing campaign was able to reach a large section of the game-playing public to familiarise them with *Guardians of the Galaxy*'s characters, which, at the same time, helped to generate huge pre-sales for the *Guardians* figurines.

In one sense, then, being part of Disney has given Marvel the opportunity to expand its newfound freedom, which it first gained when it stopped serving the studios as a development farm and secured more creative agency and industrial control. In the case

THIS PAGE, FROM TOP: 2014 film *Guardians of the Galaxy* was an unlikely success; the *Disney Infinity* game allows Marvel characters to mingle with beloved Disney characters (three images)

CLOCKWISE FROM BOTTOM: A Captain America toy; The Avengers in film form (two images)

of *Guardians*, the relatively unknown characters were given new life by being extended through cross-pollination with Disney's brand empire and its universe of characters. For not only did Disney's promotion of *Guardians*' characters, particularly Rocket Raccoon, help Marvel's film ambitions at the same time as add 'a new iconic character to associate' with Disney's brand image,[22] but figures like Rocket Raccoon also joined Disney's many 'prestigious (animal) characters',[23] which are, of course, internationally recognised. Moreover, in *Disney Infinity*, figurines

are placed upon a digital platform connected to the console, which then reads digital information from the figure and loads the character into the game. This combines the narrative layers of a game, giving depth and context to the characters therein, with the popular act of toy collection.[24]

These layers of narrative can also be enhanced in the sandbox mode of the game (called 'Toy Box'). In this mode, users can build their own worlds and mix and match characters from different storyworlds. For example, *Star Wars* characters and Marvel characters can interact.

From the above discussion we can see the ways Marvel properties operate in different media and markets, as well as the kinds of synergies that happen between Marvel characters and different modes of consumer activity, such as videogame playing and toy collecting. It is important to recognise that Marvel's incorporation into Disney is one of the driving forces behind this synergy, because it has aided the company's desire to draw together its characters in a brand association that can be harnessed and utilised in a number of ways. Marvel desires to coordinate its characters

> Cross-media synergy is a key part of Marvel's new approach to building revenue out of its characters, which ... involves constructing a cinematic universe of sequels, spin-offs and serial narratives, at the same time as developing tie-ins and storyworlds that are part of, but also separate from, this universe.

so that they reaffirm and strengthen the company's image in multiple productions, although cultivating its core brand identities – its characters – through other brand images, such as Disney's, also means that the personas and identities of characters associated with the Marvel brand are not necessarily stable (in principle, though, this is not a new situation for Marvel, a point that will be discussed in more detail shortly).[25] Cross-media synergy is a key part of Marvel's new approach to building revenue out of its characters, which, as stated at the beginning of this article, involves constructing a cinematic universe of sequels, spin-offs and serial narratives, at the same time as developing tie-ins and storyworlds that are part of, but also separate from, this universe. In this sense, Marvel is a 'single commercial entity deployed across multiple mediums' and its properties are part of a transmedia franchise 'built by aggregate across disparate formats, which converge together in a fluid unity'.[26]

This idea of 'fluid unity' is particularly important because while Marvel has drawn together characters that were once unrelated to form a particular kind of shared, fictional universe, the boundaries of this universe are permeable and the worlds within it are not always fixed or stable. Beginning with *Marvel Mystery Comics* in 1940, when the Human Torch and Namor the Sub-Mariner were first seen coexisting in the same universe, and then with the first Marvel superhero team in Issue 1 of *The Fantastic Four*, which was released in 1961, Marvel has gradually developed an 'immensely complex matrix of time and space that encompasses the stories of thousands of characters'.[27] This has not only happened within the comics themselves, but also across other media. For instance, one epic storyline involving a large network of characters, *Civil War*, first published in a series of seven comic book issues from 2006 to 2007, has been carried through the Marvel Universe in not only more than 100 comics but also tie-in books. The film *Captain America: Civil War* (Anthony & Joe Russo, 2016), produced by Marvel Studios, was informed by the story, and the narrative has also been adapted for a season of the animated television series *Avengers Assemble*, developed by

FROM TOP: The X-Men and Captain America as they appear in Marvel films

Marvel Animation. On the one hand, story events such as those in *Civil War* demonstrate the way Marvel tries to coordinate its properties across different comic book titles and mediums, which, as mentioned earlier, is the result of its desire to make sure that it plays a central role in fostering narrative expansion across various technologies and markets. This should not, however, be taken to mean that the quilt that Marvel interweaves is, in the words of Michael Mallory, 'solid'.[28] For, in the Marvel Universe, characters' backstories are 'open for continuous embellishments, additions, even outright reversals',[29] past story events can be altered or erased ('retconning'), and storylines can be simplified or restarted.

For example, the Marvel Cinematic Universe, which 'refers to the particular iteration of familiar Marvel characters that has unfolded, in an organized and ostensibly seamless continuity on screen since the release of *Iron Man* in 2008',[30] has wiped away decades of narrative history. In part it has done this in order to simplify the storyworlds for viewers discovering Marvel characters for the first time at the cinema, who otherwise might find the history that has been accrued by the Marvel Universe too difficult to navigate and, if casual viewers, might only see some of the movies or see them all but not in order. For decades it has been the job of different key personnel in the company to try to manage the timelines and other intricacies of Marvel's large textual universe to make sure readers can follow the story threads. Part of this management in the era of the Marvel Cinematic Universe involves ensuring audiences that aren't familiar with the comic books are not alienated from the work and that the mixed-viewing behaviour of multiplex audiences is accounted for. For audiences who are dedicated to seeing the movies in order but are not familiar with the comics, Marvel has also reset the serial continuity of its universe so that such viewers can follow and understand the way story and plot elements are interlinked across the films without having to know the backstories that Marvel comics fans do.

Moreover, the border that encompasses the shared, fictional universe the Marvel characters inhabit is not impenetrable. Rather, it is porous, meaning that content can move from inside to outside of the Marvel Universe (referring to all media products considered intellectual property of Marvel) and vice versa. For instance, *Spider-Man 3*, a Sony-Columbia production, is informed by an event that begins in *Secret Wars*, a twelve-issue comic book series published by Marvel from 1984 to 1985. This event has to do with a new costume that Spider-Man acquires, which turns out to be a sentient alien.

While the unity of the Marvel Universe is fluid rather than solid, many of the characters who inhabit this universe have had their stories and identities expanded across different media. As mentioned earlier, this means that alterations may occur to the look, feel and even mythology of certain characters as they are transposed across different productions. For certain audiences, such as fans of the comics who have been in it for the long haul, and who feel they have ownership over how the comics are adapted to other media, this may pose challenges to what is accepted as legitimate or traditional ways of presenting particular characters. However, it should also be remembered that while Marvel's licensing arrangements with companies like Disney have introduced a new form of brand synergy, Marvel's properties have been reinvented and remediated in the past. Moreover, it is important to recognise the role subjective perception and knowledge play in the experience that spectators have of narrative expansion. For instance, what for one audience member may appear to be a contained narrative event – say, the plot point in *Captain America: The First Avenger* of the Red Skull (Hugo Weaving) being an earlier, imperfect version of the super-soldier – may for another be read in terms of a large amount of background exposition, such as the story of Captain America's origins, which has been reinterpreted across different media over the decades (beginning with the 1979 made-for-television movie that jettisoned the mythology established in the comics). Narrative events may even be read with or against other specific texts – the plot point mentioned above, for instance, is taken directly from the 1990 film *Captain America*, which itself was a reimagining of the origin story first published in 1941. In other words, the Marvel Universe expands in different senses.

The reasons for such expansion are not purely industrial and commercial. For instance, organisational factors to do with the creative talents and desires of individual personnel working at Marvel and other companies involved in the production of Marvel or Marvel-related texts also shape the way content in the Marvel Universe is assembled to form a mutable, cross-media 'unity'. Nonetheless, the kinds of industrial factors to do with character licensing and control, development and release schedules, and company partnerships that this article has discussed determine what kinds of stories Marvel tells as well as how it tells them. These are not the only factors that shape Marvel's story universe, but they are crucial to understanding how the company's recent ambition for a large-scale form of integrated, convergent storytelling that builds on franchise logic unfolds across various media and platforms.

https://clickv.ie/w/screen-ed/marvel-films

Dr Tyson Wils teaches media at Deakin University and works as a researcher in the School of Media and Communication at RMIT University. He is the co-editor of the book Activist Film Festivals: Towards a Political Subject *(2016) and has published pieces on a range of topics including media industries, film authorship, landscape and cinema, and filmmakers including Werner Herzog, Klaus Kinski, Terrence Malick, Dario Argento and James Wan.* **SE**

Endnotes

[1] Michael Mallory, *Marvel: The Characters and Their Universe*, Hugh Lauter Levin Associates, Inc., Fairfield, CT, 2002, p. 27.
[2] Martin Flanagan, Mike McKenny & Andy Livingstone, *The Marvel Studios Phenomenon: Inside a Transmedia Universe*, Bloomsbury Academic, New York & London, 2016, pp. 23–4.
[3] ibid., p. 24.
[4] Derek Johnson, 'Cinematic Destiny: Marvel Studios and the Trade Stories of Industrial Convergence', *Cinema Journal*, vol. 52, no. 1, Fall 2012, p. 9.
[5] ibid., p. 1.
[6] Robert G Weiner, Robert Moses Peaslee & Matthew J McEniry, 'Introduction', in McEniry, Peaslee & Weiner (eds), *Marvel Comics into Film: Essays on Adaptations Since the 1940s*, McFarland & Company, Inc., Jefferson, NC, 2016, p. 2.
[7] Johnson, op. cit., p. 10.
[8] ibid.
[9] ibid., p. 9.
[10] ibid., p. 11.
[11] ibid.
[12] Flanagan, McKenny & Livingstone, op. cit., p. 28.
[13] Johnson, op. cit., p. 11.
[14] Joseph Calandro, 'Disney's Marvel Acquisition: A Strategic Financial Analysis', *Strategy & Leadership*, vol. 38, no. 2, 2010, p. 44.
[15] ibid., p. 47.
[16] Flanagan, McKenny & Livingstone, op. cit., p. 167.
[17] Weiner, Peaslee & McEniry, op. cit., p. 2.
[18] Flanagan, McKenny & Livingstone, op. cit., p. 137.
[19] Marc Graser, 'How Marvel Guards Its Properties but Isn't Afraid to Take Chances with Its *Galaxy*', *Variety*, 23 July 2014, <http://variety.com/2014/film/news/marvel-studios-guardians-of-the-galaxy-risk-1201266165/>, accessed 11 April 2017.
[20] Marc Graser, '*Guardians of the Galaxy* to Break Records for *Disney Infinity*', *Variety*, 11 September 2014, <http://variety.com/2014/digital/games/guardians-of-the-galaxy-breaks-records-for-disney-infinity-exclusive-1201302907/>, accessed 11 April 2017.
[21] Lisa Richwine & Malathi Nayak, 'Disney Sees *Infinity* Game's Retail Sales Hitting $1 Billion', *Reuters*, 12 June 2014, <http://www.reuters.com/article/us-disney-interactive-idUSKBN0EN2NM20140613>, accessed 11 April 2017.
[22] Flanagan, McKenny & Livingstone, op. cit., p. 146.
[23] ibid.
[24] ibid., p. 235.
[25] ibid., p. 27.
[26] ibid., p. 29.
[27] Mallory, op. cit., p. 13.
[28] ibid.
[29] ibid., p. 15.
[30] Flanagan, McKenny & Livingstone, op. cit., p. 6.

Light Through the DARKNESS

Using CAMELS to Analyse Steve McQueen's *Hunger*

JEREMY GUZMAN explores how Steve McQueen expertly uses the language of cinema to tell this harrowing true story of Irish activist Bobby Sands and his plight during the 1981 hunger strike.

HISTORICAL CONTEXT

Northern Ireland, 1981. There is civil unrest and political conflict as the unionists/loyalists want to stay in the United Kingdom and, in opposition to them, the nationalists/republicans want to seek independence. It is a violent time and thousands of people are dying amid the conflict. This era in Irish history is known as 'the Troubles'.

The Provisional Irish Republican Army (IRA) was a large paramilitary organisation whose mission was to form an independent republic encompassing all of Ireland. During the Troubles, which extended from the late 1960s through to 1998, the IRA secretly planned bombing campaigns on and assassinations of prison officers. As a result, in 1976 the government implemented a new policy in which the prisons in Northern Ireland no longer permitted their paramilitary prisoners to hold Special Category (or political) Status and, instead, anyone who was sentenced to jail for a Troubles-related crime was forced to wear a uniform and complete prison chores like any other criminal. Further to this, they were required to serve their time in a new prison called the Maze Prison. The prisoners reacted to this policy by refusing to wear a uniform and clothing themselves with a blanket instead, which led to the 'blanket protest'.

The tension between the prisoners and the prison authorities escalated in the following years and saw an increase in the number of assaults by prison officers. In 1978, the prisoners began to feel unsafe leaving their cells to access the bathrooms so they requested to have their own showers in their cells, which was denied. Tensions quickly grew and, as punishment for not cooperating with the authorities, the prisoners had their cells stripped of furniture and all they were left with were a blanket and a mattress to sleep on. In protest, the prisoners decided to never leave their cells, which eventuated in all of their human waste building up because the officers could not enter their rooms and remove the waste. This became known as the 'dirty protest'.

In 1980, as an attempt to regain political status, a group of republican prisoners went on a hunger strike and challenged the government to grant them the 'Five Demands':

1. The right not to wear a prison uniform.
2. The right not to do prison work.
3. The right of free association with other prisoners, and to organise educational and recreational pursuits.
4. The right to one visit, one letter and one parcel per week.
5. Full restoration of remission lost through the protest.

With no cooperation from the British government, which was now led by Margaret Thatcher, a second hunger strike was organised by IRA prisoner Bobby Sands. Sands and his fellow inmates protested against Thatcher's refusal to recognise them as political prisoners who deserve more rights.

ANALYSING *HUNGER*

The events that culminated in the 1981 hunger strike are depicted in *Hunger*, a British–Irish film released in 2008. Directed and co-written by Steve McQueen and starring Michael Fassbender as Bobby Sands, the historical drama tells the true story of Sands during his final days in the Maze Prison. It also focuses on the effects of the turmoil within the prison from the perspective of another republican prisoner, Davey Gillen (Brian Milligan),

FROM LEFT: The light filters through the prison windows; Davey (Brian Milligan)

> McQueen has the ability to express a range of ideas and emotions through poetic imagery. *Hunger* addresses many themes and ideas through the skilful employment of camera, acting, mise en scène, editing, lighting and sound.

and a prison officer, Raymond Lohan (Stuart Graham). *Hunger* received worldwide critical acclaim and won the prestigious Caméra d'Or at the Cannes Film Festival as well as a coveted BAFTA (for Most Promising Newcomer).

Possibly due to his background in video and visual art, McQueen has the ability to express a range of ideas and emotions through poetic imagery. *Hunger* addresses many themes and ideas through the skilful employment of camera, acting, mise en scène, editing, lighting and sound (CAMELS), particularly the notion of freedom as well as the contrasting notions of pain versus beauty and chaos versus order.

Camera

McQueen often frames Raymond's hands in close-up. These shots highlight the significance of the prison officer's bruised and battered hands, conveying power and control, which the audience soon realises are the causes of the conflict between the prisoners and the officers. McQueen's flair for visual storytelling is clear when he again uses a close-up to draw the audience's attention to Davey trying to catch a fly on his finger. The shot lingers for a while to illustrate the character's desire for freedom.

The idea of beauty versus pain is symbolised in an extreme close-up of snow falling on Raymond's damaged hands. This shot mirrors the inner conflict Raymond is feeling; it is implied that his tough exterior is merely a facade as he actually finds his job to be

THIS PAGE: Michael Fassbender as Bobby Sands and Liam Cunningham as Father Moran

a painful burden. McQueen reinforces this aspect of Raymond's character in the way he frames him sitting in the break room. The asymmetrical framing and negative space communicate to the audience that Raymond is an outsider among his colleagues, and that he is detached from his surroundings. The shot of Davey sitting in his cell is framed in the same way, and suggests that he, too, is alone and subdued.

McQueen often uses camera movement to immerse the audience in the world of *Hunger*. For example, a tracking shot follows Raymond when he arrives to work, which leads the audience into the Maze Prison, and a point-of-view shot from Davey's perspective places viewers in his position as he looks around his cell for the first time.

Acting

One of the most memorable scenes in *Hunger* is the seventeen-minute continuous take of a conversation between Bobby and Father Moran (Liam Cunningham) as they debate the morality of the hunger strike. Fassbender and Cunningham use a range

leans forward on the table, almost as if he is about to make an attack. Cunningham, on the other hand, portrays Father Moran as someone who is comfortable and assured. This is exhibited through the way he positions his body and sits back in the chair with his legs crossed.

> Fassbender portrays Bobby as a confident and determined individual through his posture ... Cunningham, on the other hand, portrays Father Moran as someone who is comfortable and assured.

of acting techniques to express the thoughts and emotions of their respective characters. Fassbender portrays Bobby as a confident and determined individual through his posture; he

As the tension increases between Bobby and Father Moran, Fassbender and Cunningham manipulate their voices and use gestures to communicate the characters' growing impatience with each other. They speak faster and in more assertive tones when they raise their arguments and object to the other person's opinion. At times, they point at each other when accusing their opponent of being wrong. These constant shifts in behaviour demonstrate the power play between Bobby and Father Moran, and mirror the larger conflict in the narrative. After Bobby recounts his story about the foal, it is clear that he will not back down on his decision to go on a hunger strike. Fassbender's resolute facial expressions also indicate this message to the audience. Cunningham remains silent and lets out a soft sigh to convey Father Moran's feeling of defeat. This is coupled with a straight face and furrowed eyebrows, which emphasise the character's bitter loss and disappointment. He even struggles to look at Bobby. Father Moran's admission of defeat is summed up in his parting words to Bobby: 'I don't think I'm going to see you again.'

Mise en scène

Bobby's state of mind and the theme of desolation are encapsulated in a single frame through carefully selected visual details. When Bobby sits in his cell smoking a cigarette, the frame is composed as a wide shot at eye level so that the audience sees the character's surroundings: the walls are stained with human excrement and the floor is furnished with a single mattress. The dirty, empty environment that Bobby is forced to live in contributes to *Hunger*'s desolate, bleak mood. The low-key lighting in the shot also enhances this feeling.

The asymmetrical framing and negative space within the shot work in tandem with costume to illustrate the notion of isolation; Bobby, half-clothed with just some bed linen, appears powerless and alone with only his thoughts to keep him occupied. McQueen has directed Fassbender to sit cross-legged and to look despondently past the camera. The actor's posture, paired with his facial expressions, displays Bobby's contemplative and subdued nature. While the character's surroundings are dreary, the warm orange colour that tinges the small amount of light in the room conveys the impression of comfort and security; inside his cell, Bobby is protected from his adversaries, namely the politicians and the authorities, who control the outside world. In this example of mise en scène, it is evident that McQueen's directorial choices help the audience identify with a character's mental and emotional state, as well as understand themes that are pertinent to the narrative.

Conflicted prison officer Raymond Lohan (Stuart Graham)

The Maze Prison is presented as a cold, desolate environment

Editing

A variety of editing techniques are used in *Hunger* to communicate ideas and reveal information to the audience. This is exemplified in the opening montage of Raymond getting ready for work, which depicts the mundane routine he carries out every morning. The audience understands that Raymond is someone who appreciates order and procedure, but the cut to a close-up of Raymond brushing away crumbs that have fallen on his lap implies that the character is imperfect and has something to hide. A shot of Raymond laughing with his colleagues immediately cuts to a shot of him grimacing in pain, which again suggests to the viewer that the character is putting on a facade. In these instances, the audience sees two different personas and question whether or not Raymond is an inherently violent man.

Another example of information being revealed through editing occurs during the scene in which Bobby receives his new prison uniform. Here, the camera establishes that the uniform is on the bed then cuts to a close-up of Bobby's leg fidgeting, illustrating his restlessness, frustration and rage building up. The hunger strike conversation between Bobby and Father Moran plays out in a single take to create the impression that the audience is observing two opponents battle each other, as in a game of chess. The film cuts to a close-up of Bobby when he begins to tell the story about the foal, which engages the audience and draws viewers in

THIS SPREAD: Emaciated prisoners struggle to survive during the hunger strike

to what he is saying. The film cuts to Father Moran only once during the entire scene, which emphasises the overwhelming impact of Bobby's words.

Jump cuts are used in the film to build tension and anxiety. This is evident when Bobby is being dragged through the prison and the combination of jump cuts with fast-paced editing creates a feeling of discomfort and franticness. Similarly, jump cuts are employed when Bobby and the inmates demolish their cells to convey resentment and hostility.

Cross dissolves are used conventionally to indicate that time has passed, as when a shot of Bobby at night-time sitting in front of a fire overlaps with a shot of Bobby in the morning looking out the window. The same technique is utilised when Bobby's uneaten trays of food are being replaced; from this, the audience knows that Bobby is enduring the hunger strike.

Slow motion and juxtaposition are employed to convey meaning to the viewer. During the riot scene, the police are attacking Bobby in slow motion on one side of the frame and a distressed lone police officer is seen at normal speed on the other side of the frame. The editing in this scene emphasises the incessant agony that the men are experiencing. In the film's closing sequence, a shot of Bobby shedding a tear and taking one final breath is juxtaposed with a shot of birds flying away to symbolise Bobby's death and subsequent freedom.

Lighting

Details about the character of Bobby are also revealed through the film's lighting design. The backlighting in the shot that shows Bobby looking out the window in his cell creates a silhouette and displays a sense of mystery, as the audience is aware that he is conspiring against the prison officers. Intrigue and secrecy are further implied by the under-lighting of Bobby, whose face is hidden in shadows. At this moment, the audience is pondering what he has planned to do next.

The scenes in which Bobby is lying on his deathbed are constructed with high-key lighting and a blue-grey tint to convey the cold and sterile environment of the prison infirmary. The lighting also connotes that he is exposed and vulnerable. Conversely, when Bobby is having visions of his younger self during his final moments, the infirmary is illuminated with a warm orange tint to illustrate comfort and security; Bobby feels at peace as he remembers his childhood. In the shot that shows young Bobby (Ciaran Flynn) standing over his future self, the expressive lighting is low-key, evoking the feeling of gloom. The darkness surrounding young Bobby suggests to the audience that he represents the grim reaper and Bobby's impending death. In the background of this shot is a window emitting bright white light, which is a recurring motif in the film. This natural light symbolises hope and freedom, both of which are key themes in *Hunger*; Bobby is sacrificing his life to attain an intangible freedom and give his fellow republicans hope in their battle for justice.

Sound

The sense of chaos and anarchy is present right from the beginning of *Hunger*, as in the diegetic sound of rubbish-bin lids banging on the footpath. In contrast, a feeling of peace and stillness is instilled in the audience when Raymond is outside in the snow and only the soft breeze can be heard. Non-diegetic sound is also used to convey emotions in the film: melancholic and sorrowful music underscores the scene in which Bobby is carried away to his cell after being mistreated by the prison officers, which further highlights Bobby's defeat and anguish.

Sound is altered and edited to immerse the audience in the narrative. For example, the diegetic sounds of punches being thrown at the prisoners are amplified to accentuate the pain and brutality they are experiencing. During the riot scene, in which one of the prisoners is being beaten up by a police officer, the sound gradually cuts out to place the audience in the character's situation and audibly express the sensation of losing consciousness. The diegetic sounds intensify and become rhythmic when Bobby and the inmates demolish their cells, yelling aggressively and throwing furniture at the walls. The construction of sound during this moment in the film builds tension and creates anarchy. This notion is reinforced when the riot police scream and repeatedly strike their batons in unison against their shields.

Non-simultaneous sound can be heard as Thatcher speaks about the prisoners seeking pity while the camera tracks over the wet prison floor. The pairing of the dialogue and visuals symbolises bloodshed and the damaging impact of the prisoners' actions.

As Bobby is lying on his deathbed, only faint breaths can be heard and the sound is bare, which conveys the feeling of fragility and lifelessness. The sound mixing suggests to the audience that Bobby is nearing death and becoming disconnected from reality as the audio of the visitor talking to him is muffled and the fluorescent light hums in the background. Conversely, sound instils

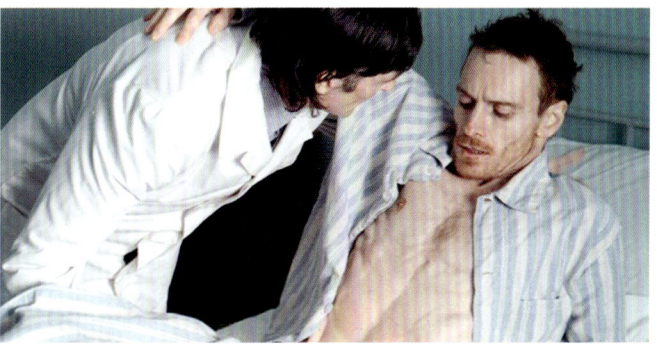

a sense of life and existence into the narrative when Bobby relives his childhood in a flashback: the diegetic sounds are vibrant and busy as children chant and laugh on a bus driving along the countryside. The score at the end of the sequence, which can be characterised as strings sustaining the same notes that slowly fade away and eventually disappear, signifies Bobby hanging onto the final moments of his life, and his life tragically ending.

* * *

Steve McQueen is a visual storyteller who uses minimal dialogue and exposition, relying more on the technical elements of filmmaking to construct narrative, mood and emotion. He expertly utilises the medium of film to communicate various themes and ideas, to prompt reflection among viewers, and to fully immerse them in the world that his characters exist in.

https://clickv.ie/w/screen-ed/hunger

Jeremy Guzman is currently the head of visual arts at Marymede Catholic College where he teaches Media and Drama. Graduating from Swinburne University of Technology with a Bachelor of Film and Television, Jeremy also writes, directs and produces for the screen and stage. **SE**

Active Audiences

Lessons on Media Agency and Control

Teaching theory can be dry at the best of times – but it doesn't have to be. **DEBORAH SPILSBURY** recounts how she prompted her Year 12 students to enthusiastically learn and engage by getting them to put media theories into action in the school community.

This piece refers to Unit 4, Area of Study 3 of the current VCE Media study design (2012–2017), but much of the content will likely be relevant to Unit 4, Area of Study 2 of the new VCE Media study design (2018–2022).

ALL IMAGES: Screenshots from student project 'grATAR than the ATAR'

There is no doubt that Media students are a creative bunch. As a Media teacher, I am always inspired by the mix of students that I am presented with at the beginning of every year. In almost all cases, they have chosen Media because they have a desire to create something, whether it be a thought-provoking photographic series, a short film or some other media-production piece. They are also fairly media-savvy as far as their use and consumption of the media goes – or at least they think they are – and are usually keen to discuss and share their opinions on anything media-related.

Their media production is often their driving force and, after a wonderful few weeks in the world of 'Narrative', armed with their technical know-how and a complete production design plan, they are keen to launch themselves into their production work without too much cajoling from me.

By August, however, the wheels are usually starting to slow as the end of their production work is in sight. Signs of fatigue begin to show as the demands of Year 12 increase and the students set their sights on the finish line.

It is perhaps not surprising, then, that as I found myself introducing the final area of study in Unit 4, 'Media influence', I watched the colour draining collectively from the faces of the students and detected a slight groan emanating from one corner of the room. At this stage, the students are completely unaware that the unit is about to get content-heavy and it is thus up to me, who does know, to inject as much vigour and enthusiasm into the next few weeks of learning as possible.

The VCE Media study design outlines the 'key knowledge' requirements as follows:

- *communication theories and models and their application to media forms and texts*
- *theories of audience, their relationship with communication theories and models, and application to media forms and texts*
- *arguments and evidence about media influence of audiences and the broader society*
- *arguments surrounding the rationale for and regulation of the media*
- *appropriate media language and terminology.*[1]

As is the nature of a study design, these five short dot points are in no way indicative of the scope of theory required to fully cover this area of study. Nor does it prescribe which communication theories should be studied. It does, however, state that students should be able to 'identify, compare and contrast communication theories and models'.[2] With this in mind, it is necessary to provide students with a range of theories to allow for comparison, both in terms of the nature of the influence and the extent to which the audience is likely to be affected by the messages received.

As Media teachers, we know that some of the communication theories of choice include the 'hypodermic needle' theory, the 'reinforcement' theory, the 'agenda-setting' theory, the 'two-step flow' theory and the 'uses and gratification' theory. While it is widely accepted that the hypodermic needle theory is outdated and unsound in its application, it remains an interesting communication theory to share with students. It posits that the media has a powerful influence over its audience, and if nothing else provides an excellent basis of comparison for students as they go on to study later theories. Students are able to not only acknowledge the suggested historical evidence in support of this theory, but also see the limitations of the theory based on their own logical understanding of the media's influence.

From the hypodermic needle theory, then, it is likely that most Media teachers, including me, start to move forward in time, introducing each new theory and proposed influence on audience. The class will explore evidence to support the validity of each

theory and, just to add a little confusion to the mix, students will be reminded repeatedly that these are just theories and that there is no definitive answer to the relationship between mass media and audience. Needless to say, this notion is often met with cries of, 'Well why are we studying it then?'

About three classes into the unit, it was time to explore the two-step flow theory, which was proposed by Paul Lazarsfeld in the 1940s in response to his research carried out during a US presidential election campaign. The theory suggests that a target audience is more likely to be influenced by messages that are diffused via people whose opinions they value. Therefore, if established opinion leaders deliver a message through the mass media, then this message is more likely to influence the target audience.

The two-step flow theory is one of the more entertaining of the communication theories to study, as students make connections to their own experiences of the media relatively easily. Examples of viral campaigns that have benefitted from opinion leaders include the ice-bucket challenge,[3] Kony 2012[4] and #IStandWithAdam,[5] which all used celebrities and other prominent individuals to deliver messages through the media.

As I began introducing the two-step flow theory, I looked out at what was usually a vision of bright and happy students, only to see a sea of tired faces, some with eyelids drooping, and I realised that I needed to do something to engage this group of young people. I needed to find a way to turn a unit of work from what currently felt like wading through a theoretical quagmire into something that would be relevant and meaningful, and would above all tap back into these creative minds.

I needed to find a way to turn a unit of work from what currently felt like wading through a theoretical quagmire into something that would be relevant and meaningful.

THEORY INTO PRACTICE: THE CHALLENGE

Despite the pressing demands on time, I decided to take a risk and challenge the class to put their current understanding of communication theory into practice via a whole-class project.

The project would involve producing a media campaign using opinion leaders to deliver a message with the intent to influence a target audience. In other words, to put the two-step flow theory into action. The target audience prescribed was 'Year 12 students', and it was up to the class to brainstorm a campaign focus, which could be any topical message suitable for this age group. Based on the target audience and campaign focus, the next step was to select opinion leaders within this target group who would then endorse and deliver the campaign message.

As I outlined the project to the class, the atmosphere in the room immediately sprang to life as the students began to discuss what type of campaign they wanted to deliver. After some time and much deliberation over a number of topical issues, they decided to focus on the increasing anxiety around their imminent VCE exams and the resulting ATAR scores, something that they and their peers were becoming acutely aware of and concerned about. Many of them felt distressed by the fact that the sum of their educational years was about to be reduced to an ATAR score, when they really wanted to be defined by the full and rounded experiences, opportunities and successes they had all had throughout their college lives.

They quite quickly came up with their campaign slogan: 'Be grATAR than the ATAR'.

The students then began to think about the opinion leaders that would deliver the message. They realised that in order to maximise the influence of the campaign message, they would need to select students from across the cohort whose interests and friendship groups reflected all of their peers. They also wanted to include students with recognised leadership roles and to ask the Head of Senior School to deliver a short message of encouragement.

The next discussion revolved around the delivery of the campaign. It was decided that the campaign would be in the form of a short video in which the opinion leaders would deliver the clear message, 'We are more than just a number' by answering the question, 'Why are you greater than the ATAR?' For maximum impact and exposure, the campaign would remain under wraps until the Year 12 end-of-year assembly, at which the whole senior school would be present. After this, it would be uploaded to YouTube and shared by three students through Facebook.

The final part of the challenge was to decide how we would measure the success of the campaign. We decided that we would use the hits on the YouTube video as our measure of influence. Assuming our opinion leaders had done their job, we determined that we would be satisfied if the video received at least 500 views, as this would be more than double our Year 12 cohort. Although a little rudimentary, this would satisfy the premise of our two-step flow theory experiment.

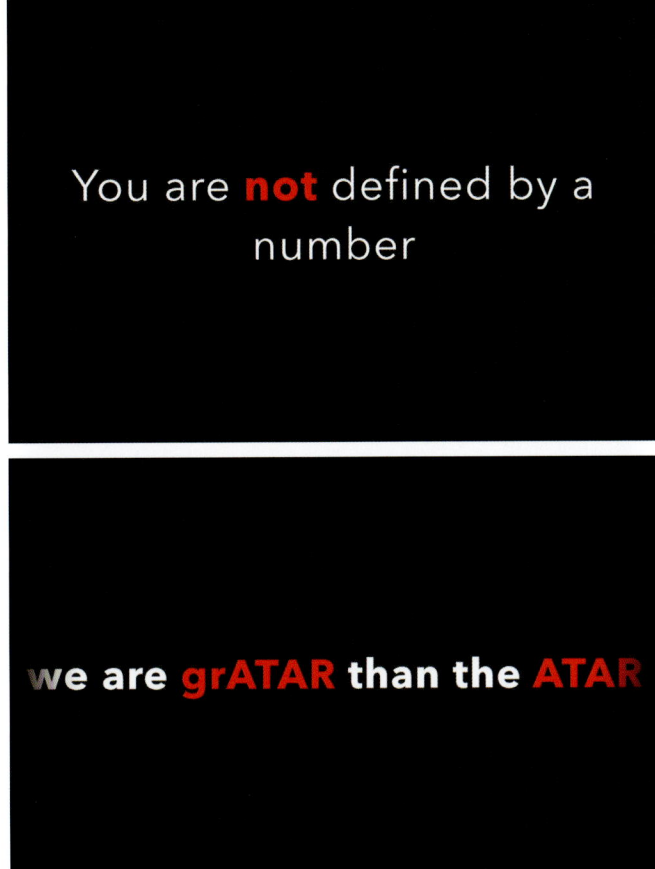

Assuming our opinion leaders had done their job, we determined that we would be satisfied if the video received at least 500 views ... this would satisfy the premise of our two-step flow theory experiment.

CAMPAIGN DEVELOPMENT AND LAUNCH

Suffice it to say, the dynamics of the classroom changed from then on: among the continuing digestion of theory, analysis and discussion there was a buzz of activity as the class began the process of campaign development.

To meet the time constraints, the technical aspects of the campaign were kept to a minimum, with a corner of the studio set up with a video camera and a plain black background. This allowed for the opinion leaders and the Head of Senior School to drop by when they were free over the course of a couple of weeks to film their response to the campaign question. After the final interview had taken place, a core group of students began the editing process in preparation for the deadline of the Year 12 assembly.

The morning of the assembly finally arrived. Emotions were running high as the senior school students filed into the hall. The Year 12 celebration is always a heartfelt occasion as students reminisce over their time at the college through a series of entertaining items and genuine reflection. As the 'grATAR than the ATAR' video played, there was a palpable hush that descended over the audience and there were many – staff and students alike – who could be seen quietly wiping away a tear as the students in the video shared their thoughts about what made them 'more than just a number'.

The timing of the campaign launch had been perfect; it was evident that the Media students had managed to encapsulate a very real issue pertaining to their target audience with this three-minute video. Straight after the assembly, the video was uploaded to YouTube and the three core students put the link onto their Facebook pages.

Then, we waited!

RESULTS

Within a few hours, we had reached our initial goal of 500 YouTube hits. The students excitedly shared emails and texts as the views increased and the interest began to build. It appeared that the campaign, and our opinion leaders, had struck a chord with the wider community: over the next few days we discovered that two schools had shared the video in their own assemblies, and one school had used the video in their Media class as a basis for their own study of media influence.

From then on, the campaign grew legs of its own and spread beyond the bounds of our immediate community. By the following week, two of the students had been contacted by the radio and the local press and asked to be interviewed about the project. It was at this point that we all realised that what had begun as a class project had become a bona fide campaign that had already reached an audience more than 300 kilometres away.

As my students prepared for the radio and newspaper interviews, we were able to discuss the fluidity of the communication theories we had studied, as we now seemed to be moving into the realms of the agenda-setting theory (the notion that the news media has the power to influence by deciding which stories are presented to the public and thereby creating interest in and a discourse around this topic) and the reinforcement theory (which posits that audiences will be more likely to accept and support an idea if it already aligns with their pre-existing values). The interest from the radio and the newspaper added an extra dimension to our research, as we were able to show a spike in audience interest through the YouTube hits after the local newspaper article had been released. Immediately following this, Melbourne newspaper the *Herald Sun* picked up the campaign, featuring it in an online article and increasing the number of hits to 5005 – all this in just under two weeks of the launch date. Observing the increase in YouTube hits after the campaign was covered in the media, in particular the national newspaper, created an interesting class discussion around the influence of media organisations and their role as 'gatekeepers' to information consumed by the masses, and the general discourse generated about the campaign focus both within the school community and through reading the online interest also made the class think about how pre-existing beliefs may influence how the campaign is received by certain audience types.

It was incredibly rewarding to observe my students moving from the academic study of Media in the classroom to becoming influential opinion leaders themselves, and engaging directly with the theories and the media organisations that they were studying.

EVALUATION

It would be fair to say that in evaluating the project, the class felt that they exceeded their expectations in terms of exploring the possibilities of creating a sphere of influence using the media and the premise of the two-step flow theory. I wholeheartedly agreed and had I attached a grade to this project, which ironically would have contradicted the campaign focus absolutely, I would have gladly given every one of them top marks. The project was not about grades, however, but rather about engagement, and perhaps

The class felt that they exceeded their expectations in terms of exploring the possibilities of creating a sphere of influence using the media and the premise of the two-step flow theory.

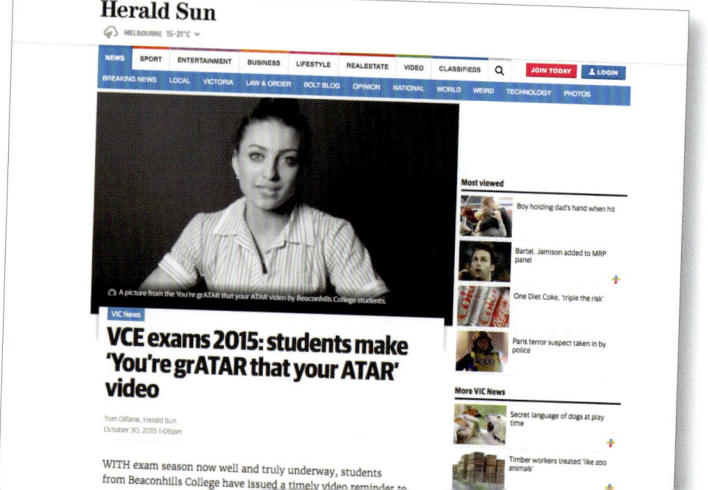

the most rewarding aspects for me were the learning opportunities that I could not have anticipated.

Students were actively learning throughout the project, and as each opportunity presented itself, discussions naturally flowed in terms of how we were going to respond to the growing interest in the campaign. The learning that took place in terms of media influence, communication and audience theories was real, as the students were able to make connections between their own experience and the theories they were exploring.

Taking a content-heavy unit of work and incorporating a practical element, albeit with a little trepidation so late in the year, turned

LEFT: The project was featured in the *Herald Sun*

what was potentially going to be an uphill climb towards the Year 12 examinations into a class of students who were re-energised, enthusiastic and, above all, engaging actively with the course material.

As the flurry of excitement dissipated and we turned our attention to revision and the examinations, the number of hits on the video continued to slowly rise; at the time of writing, it has been viewed over 7000 times. While this project is perhaps now just a satisfying memory in the minds of the students in this class, the campaign message remains with those in our school community who were part of the experience. And who knows, if the core group of students had wanted to take the campaign further, then perhaps their message would still be active and part of the growing discourse as to whether a number alone can truly be indicative of a student's academic performance and ability.

As I reflect on my own teaching practice, this experience has confirmed to me the importance of continually responding to the class dynamic and to the group of students who are collectively unique each year. Even when, on the face of it, a unit of study looks like it can only be taught one way, flipping the classroom and allowing the students to take control over the learning process not only raised their interest and energy levels but also increased the breadth of the learning taking place overall. In this particular case, the practical task enabled this group of enthusiastic, creative and collaborative Media students to engage actively in this area of study to achieve their outcomes, and also provided an enriching and memorable learning experience for both the students and their teacher.

Deborah Spilsbury is a teacher of Media at Beaconhills College, Melbourne. **SE**

Endnotes

1. Victorian Curriculum and Assessment Authority, VCE Media study design (2012–2017), 2011, available at <http://www.vcaa.vic.edu.au/Documents/vce/media/media-sd-2012.pdf>, accessed 13 April 2017, p. 29.
2. ibid.
3. See Nicky Woolf, 'Remember the Ice Bucket Challenge? It Just Funded an ALS Breakthrough', *The Guardian*, 27 July 2016, <https://www.theguardian.com/society/2016/jul/26/ice-bucket-challenge-als-charity-gene-discovery>, accessed 13 April 2017.
4. See Christina Cauterucci, 'The Lessons of Kony 2012', *Slate*, 16 September 2016, <http://www.slate.com/articles/news_and_politics/the_next_20/2016/09/kony_2012_quickly_became_a_punch_line_but_what_if_it_did_more_good_than.html>, accessed 13 April 2017.
5. See Deborah Gough, '#istandwithadam: Social Media Campaign Rallies for Sydney Swans Star Adam Goodes', *The Age*, 1 August 2015, <http://www.theage.com.au/afl/afl-news/istandwithadam-social-media-campaign-rallies-for-sydney-swans-star-adam-goodes-20150731-gip9p9.html>, accessed 13 April 2017.

PACKING A PUNCH
Structuring a Short Comedy Film

Making a short comedy film can seem like an easy task – throw a few gags in, maybe some slapstick, and you've got a movie worthy of Funny or Die, right? As VINCENT PICKERING explains, though, it's a little more complicated than that, but with some careful planning and attention to narrative structure, students can create truly great – and hilarious – pieces of work.

Comedy is a favourite genre of many film students, but it can be very hard to pull off. And while many books have been published to assist filmmakers in creating engaging short films, beyond recognition as a dominant genre or useful device,[1] comedy is rarely touched on. As there aren't many resources focusing on the effective writing of short comedy films, students are frequently left to rely on their own instincts when it comes to comedy filmmaking. This all too often results in what is essentially a short drama film that has humorous elements, and/or films littered with in-jokes, wacky accents, absurd props, zany costumes and a blooper reel that lasts longer than the actual film. *Shudder.* Here, I outline a strategy for comedy writing that will help students to design effective short comedy films by applying a narrative structure that builds the humour to a climax, and which will in turn save students from continuing to be disappointed when their film doesn't achieve its comedic goals.

THE SHORT COMEDY GENRE

The short comedy harks back to the earliest use of film. Indeed, the earliest known scripted (fictional) film ever made is thought to be Louis Lumière's forty-five-second silent slapstick *L'arroseur arrosé* from 1895. Telling a story in front of the camera revolutionised the industry, which was then taken further by Georges Méliès. These days, the majority of short films are produced by amateur, independent and student filmmakers who are looking to hone, showcase and promote their skills, with the hope that such films will lead to future work. Filmmakers often rely on the appeal of the short comedy, particularly when entering film competitions and festivals[2] such as Tropfest, which for the last seven years has been won by films with comedic elements.

COMEDY WRITING

In writing a short comedy film, it is useful to deconstruct how comedy itself is commonly structured. When considering the set-up for, and structure of, jokes with a punchline, along with how a stand-up comedian structures their set to deliver their strongest material at the end, it becomes clear that many effective comedy films also end in a comedic climax. The first two acts contain elements that are often disguised as smaller jokes (or appear close to smaller jokes), but which serve primarily to set up a big laugh in the final act. This is also a trademark of many successful episodes of *Seinfeld* (more on this later), with each of the characters' storylines 'dovetailing' at the end to create a sum greater than its individual parts.[3]

FILM WRITING

Infamous film structure proponents such as Robert McKee,[4] Blake Snyder[5] and Syd Field[6] describe paradigms whose three-act formats build to a final climax, and structuring a short comedy film with this in mind is extremely beneficial. Character development is just as crucial for a short comedy film, and breaking down the comedic elements and their purpose enables the writer to time and build the humour for maximum effect. An understanding of three-act narrative structure allows the filmmaker to ensure that their audience, accustomed to stories with the orientation–complication–resolution format, are more likely to understand and get the most out of the intended humour in the film.

It is not assumed that all short comedy films follow the 'comedic climax' structure, but this describes a trend and generic structure shared by numerous short comedy films, as well as many sitcom episodes and web series. At first glance, many are quick to dismiss the structure as being that of a 'gag film' – a type of film that appears to be structured for the sole purpose of the punchline at the end – but this underestimates the prevalence of structure as a generic device in short comedy. For example, the Syd Field paradigm (right) works similarly in its breakdown of feature-length film structure in relation to the three-act structure. It is useful to consider the number and location of plot points and pinches on the timeline, which signal when important points in the narrative should take place. For example, a plot point occurs at the end of an act to propel the action into the next act. Writers can likewise determine the number of jokes and set-ups they might need to have before the comedic climax in the third act. Explicit knowledge of this foundation will allow the short comedy writer to structure their script in a way that will most effectively serve the comedy of their film.

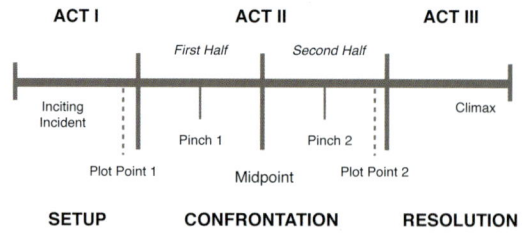

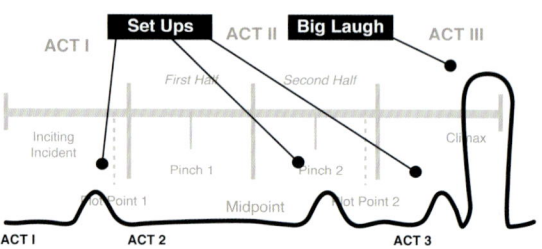

SETTING THE TONE

An important step in writing a short comedy that students are often reluctant to commit to is careful planning. In designing a short-film concept, it can be useful to first think of that final climactic humorous scenario, then work backwards, inserting and hiding the necessary elements needed for the audience to get the most humour out of the climax. The writer therefore consciously works to set up the big laugh as efficiently as possible, while also quickly orientating the audience to accept the humour by establishing the 'comic climate'[7] of the film. This refers to setting the tone of the film, warming the audience up for the style of humour being used. Consider the type of comedy you are trying to create, particularly in terms of the comedic climax – for example, absurd or slapstick – and ensure that is represented clearly to the audience and will not be missed or misinterpreted. Just as the first act orientates the audience to the who, what, why, when and where of the story, a short comedy also needs to get the audience in the right frame of mind to start looking for the humour.

INFLUENTIAL PRACTITIONERS

As short filmmaking is so often seen as a stepping stone to other formats such as television and long-form film, it is quite rare for an artist to work within the format for an extended period and therefore strongly impact on it, and perhaps establish a trend with their style. A number of narrative web series, however, have gained a following for their style and humour, and operate in a way that closely resembles the short film. At a glance, sketch comedy also closely resembles the appearance and style of a short comedy film. A comedy sketch, however, with its roots in the vaudeville era, is more centred on the joke itself rather than the filmmaking style, which is integral to short comedy films. Classic sitcoms *Seinfeld* and *Fawlty Towers* have also been highly influential, as the shows' writers consistently structured the narratives to serve the humour arc. The classic *Fawlty Towers* episode 'The Germans' climaxes with Basil's (John Cleese) hilarious goose-stepping impersonation of Adolf Hitler, but consider all of the elements that combine to make that really funny:

- Basil has an awkwardly racist conversation with the regular guest Major Gowen (Ballard Berkeley), who is still holding a grudge against the Germans from the war.
- He has a concussion so cannot fully control his impulses and is disorientated.
- He got that concussion from the fire-drill misadventure, with Manuel (Andrew Sachs) accidentally hitting him over the head with the frying pan he was using to smother the actual fire. He was also previously hit on the head by the moose.
- It is established very early in the episode that Germans are staying at the hotel, and Basil is desperately trying to make things pleasant for them and has previously instructed a few people to not 'mention the war'.
- He is trying to cheer up the crying German guest with anything he can think of, but (assumedly because of his concussion) can only think of Nazi Germany references.

The classic *Seinfeld* episode 'The Marine Biologist' ends with George's (Jason Alexander) dramatic retelling of pulling a golf ball from the blowhole of a whale. This is only possible because, firstly, Jerry (Jerry Seinfeld) erroneously tells George's date at the start of the episode that George is a marine biologist (and George has been established to be the kind of character that will just go along with the lie rather than correct it); and, secondly, again very early in the episode, Kramer (Michael Richards) explains that his new hobby is using the ocean as a driving range, and that he only gets off one good shot, which in turn sets up the final line, 'a hole in one'.

EXAMPLES OF SHORT COMEDY FILMS

The Mother Situation (Matt Day, 2016) – 2017 Tropfest winner <https://vimeo.com/204136643>

Granny Smith (Julian Lucas, 2014) – 2014 Tropfest winner <https://youtu.be/vZnSAa9Vbl0>

Long Story Short – I Went to the Bathroom (Almog Avidan Antonir, 2014) <https://youtu.be/OtF_W2EZkTE>

Lemonade Stand (Alethea Jones, 2012) – 2012 Tropfest winner <https://youtu.be/9JL82j-l6hM>

A Day in the Life of a Librarian (Benjamin Griggs, 2013) – won several 2013 BUFTAs <https://youtu.be/Mcn-B7X7HwQ>

Spider (Nash Edgerton, 2007) – 2007 Sydney Film Festival Audience Award, Best Short Film <https://youtu.be/fyhs8dKMTN4>

The above films all utilise a generic structure of building to a climactic plot and comic resolution, and thus can be used to demonstrate the comedic climax structure.

The obvious subjectivity of comedy means that this structure is not a guaranteed formula for success, and the unpredictability of inspiration also signifies that not all successful short comedy films must be constructed in this way. However, it remains a method that provides the comedy writer with a strong foundation on which to build their film.

WRITING A SHORT COMEDY FILM

Want to make a short comedy film? Well, making up your storyline and the jokes as you film may sound like fun, but more often than not, you end up wasting a lot of production time on something not nearly as funny or entertaining for your audience as if you had spent a bit of time planning it beforehand.

YOUR GOAL
A good short comedy is not only funny all the way through, but the humour builds to its funniest point at the end. Think of your overall film like a joke with the punchline at the end, but also consider how you are setting up that punchline so the audience will find it as funny as possible. The start of your film therefore needs to do a lot, as it serves to hook the audience, orientating them not only to the story, but also to what kind of humour the film is using, while also setting up the comedic climax at the end.

BRAINSTORMING YOUR ENDING
Maybe you already have a vague idea of what kind of film you want to make (for example, a detective parody or a couple breaking up), which is great. But rather than just starting to write and hoping your characters wind up somewhere funny, think the other way around: imagine a hilarious ending, then figure out what combination of events would need to happen for the characters to get there. (Maybe the detective somehow accidentally arrests himself? What sequence of events would allow for that to happen? Maybe, with the couple, the boyfriend is so upset he forgot he had timed all these grand romantic gestures to happen, ending with an explosion of balloons and confetti? How could you hint to the audience that this might be happening without giving it away?) Even the craziest scenarios can be set up in a way that both surprises the audience and stays believable. The key to a good comedic climax (and, some say, punchlines in general) is an ending that makes sense but is unexpected. Importantly, your ending does not actually need to be that clever, as it is the way that you carefully execute it that will make the audience laugh.

I CAN'T THINK OF ANYTHING!
If you are really stuck, and feel like you just can't come up with anything, the most important step is to *just start writing*. Some people work by thinking out loud and recording it, others by writing it down or typing it out. Put down every idea you have in a train-of-thought note, including any bad ideas, side jokes you might suddenly think of or lines of dialogue. For now, don't edit it at all – if you think of something better than something you wrote earlier, just add it afterwards. It might look like a big block of unusable text to anyone else who sees it, but small ideas and jokes might come out of it. The most important thing is to actually be thinking about and developing your idea. Even if it means you only come up with a bunch of ideas you know you don't want, you're still a little bit closer to the jokes or story that you *do* want.

SETTING IT UP
You need to give the audience just the right amount of information to understand the ending, but not necessarily see it coming. To do this, you need to be able to deconstruct exactly what the audience needs to know/see/hear (or often *not* know/see/hear) in order to force them to make certain assumptions and get the most out of the humour at the end of your film. For example, if your ending's comedic climax involves a character being mistaken for somebody else, then maybe to make it more believable, someone needs to comment on them having a new haircut? Small things like this will accumulate to ensure the ending makes sense, making it funnier and more authentic. You also need to consider the style of comedy you are aiming for (such as dark or gross-out), and establish that style as quickly as possible with similar jokes, not only to hook your audience and get them laughing, but also to get them in the right mood to accept that ending. Every part and line of the first and second acts should therefore serve a purpose to either further the plot, or use humour to put the audience in the right position to get the most out of the comedic climax in the third act.

COVER YOUR TRACKS
Be careful to avoid the common pitfall of obvious exposition, dialogue or plot information, by covering your tracks and blending everything in together, so that although a joke or piece of plot information is present, it does not stand out to the audience as extraneous. Fortunately, humour can be very useful to cover up any obvious plot points. In the above example, instead of having someone just mention the haircut, have them say something funny about it. You might even need to go one step further and do something earlier to set up that joke too, which will further disguise that you are really just revealing plot information or setting up your climax.

REVIEW
Writing is rewriting. Go over your script again and again, imagining you are watching your film for the first time to make sure everything is in its right place, and nothing is left up to chance or could be funnier. By the time you are ready for production, you should have a script you *know* will be funny. Sure, you might think of something even funnier in the moment, or an actor might improvise some new dialogue, but do yourself a favour and film the original stuff as well, in case you are just getting caught up in the moment and it's not really as funny when you get down to editing it.

Vincent Pickering lives, writes, teaches and jokes around in Brisbane, Qld. **SE**

Endnotes

[1] Edmond Levy, *Making a Winning Short: How to Write, Direct, Edit, and Produce a Short Film*, Owl Books, New York, 1994.
[2] See, for example, Roy Unger, quoted in Kim Adelman, *Making It Big in Shorts: The Ultimate Filmmaker's Guide to Short Films*, Michael Wiese Productions, Studio City, CA, 2004, p. 64.
[3] Todd VanDerWerff, 'Seinfeld Is Finally Streaming Online. Here Are 5 Ways It Changed Television.', *Vox*, 24 June 2015, <http://www.vox.com/2014/7/6/5874267/seinfeld-anniversary-article>, accessed 4 April 2017.
[4] See Robert McKee, *Story: Substance, Structure, Style, and the Principles of Screenwriting*, Regan Books, New York, 1997.
[5] See Blake Snyder, *Save the Cat! The Last Book on Screenwriting You'll Ever Need*, Michael Wiese Productions, Studio City, CA, 2005.
[6] See Syd Field, *Screenplay: The Foundations of Screenwriting*, revised edn, Bantam Dell, New York, 2005.
[7] See Jonathan Lyons, *Comedy for Animators*, CRC Press, Boca Raton, FL, 2016, p. 117.

ENTRIES ARE NOW OPEN!

1 MINUTE FILM COMPETITION

FOR SCHOOL STUDENTS

THIS YEAR'S THEME IS 'TOMORROW'

TO ENTER: CREATE AND SUBMIT YOUR 1-MINUTE FILM.

FOUR $500 PRIZES ARE UP FOR GRABS!

For more information, or to enter, visit

1-minutefilmcompetition.org

Entries close midday AEST, Friday 28 July 2017

The 1-Minute Film Competition 2017 is free to enter, and is open to all primary and secondary-school students in Australia and New Zealand.

Proudly presented by:

SYNC OR SWIM
ADOBE PREMIERE CLIP

KEVIN LAVERY

www.screeneducation.com.au

There is a general assumption that anyone who attended university after the year 2000 has a very particular set of skills. Skills acquired naturally through being everyone's favourite mid-2000s education buzzword, 'digital natives'.[1] That ability to be 'good with technology' or 'know computers'. They're often referred to as some portmanteau made up of a random technology term and a synonym for expert: 'Let's ask Kevin, he's our resident whizputer; our digispert; our HDMI-cordoyen.'

And this assumption comes from the same place as Marc Prensky's misunderstanding. These digital natives are *comfortable* with technology, they are *familiar* with it, they welcome its use. But comfort does not beget skill; their familiarity with digital technologies does not make them automatically skilled in their use. It's a myth.

I personally fit into the group of millennials who are both familiar with technology and reasonably adept at using it. Reasonably adept. I'm not amazing at it – I'm no David Lightman.[2] My skills have limits, but they are born of my lack of interest in taking the time necessary to expand them. The knowledge and skills I do have, I retain (and grow) through practice. Prensky was right in equating digital skills and know-how with language and culture. But, while I can use a computer to do stuff, make stuff and solve problems, I'm not necessarily the norm.[3] Millennials run the full gamut of digital skills and understanding. Digital natives are just as likely as 'digital immigrants' to be the embodiment of the bigoted immigrant parody: they haven't learnt the language, they don't try to assimilate, and they try to force everything to work in a format or style that they are comfortable with (instead of adjusting to changing social and cultural norms).

So misunderstandings, and educational writing based on misunderstandings, have got us to the point where anyone who attended university after the year 2000 is assumed to have 'the knack' when it comes to digital technology. They can write a blog, they can design a poster, they can make a website, they can make a movie, they can fix your DVD player, they can install your software, they can get you the latest episode of *Game of Thrones*, they know what VR is, they can do this guy ¯_(ツ)_/¯, and everything they own is part of the Internet of Things, just beeping and booping through life. It's like a generation of lawnmower men were born in the mid 1980s / early 1990s. A big change in education curricula at universities in the last twenty years has been that terms like 'digital' and 'PDF' are sprinkled liberally through courses and units like black cats through a Party Mix,[4] without having the requisite amount of time devoted to learning about them comprehensively. But even if you could learn about all the disparate technologies, it might not matter anyway – you could spend a whole unit on electronic whiteboards to find that they are often unavailable in schools (either through not ever being purchased or by having been permanent-markered by an absent-minded teacher). Digital literacy is like any literacy – it's not picked up through osmosis. There are the rare cases of Matilda-like geniuses who teach themselves, but for the most part it is learnt and then built on by those with an interest.

This expectation of digital know-how is compounded by an aspect of education that has been growing over the last decade, an idea that doesn't just affect the millennial teachers but all teachers: the idea of teacher as creator. Computers being proportionately favoured over textbooks, catering for a greater variety of learners as well as the increased support for flipped and blended learning approaches, has had a big effect on the teacher and their position within the curriculum. It's as if the teacher is now the centre of the curriculum. The rise of project-based learning in twenty-first century education theory has given way to an increase in production as a form of delivery rather than just a form of assessment. Today's teachers often need the same skills to synthesise the information for student delivery that students need to synthesise the information for their assessments. While this aspect of it is time-consuming, there is a lot to be said for this

Today's teachers often need the same skills to synthesise the information for student delivery that students need to synthesise the information for their assessments. While this aspect of it is time-consuming, there is a lot to be said for this approach to education.

approach to education. It is a good way to synthesise information, helps students master a lot of soft skills and collaborative workflows, and can be a big factor in the motivation to learn.[5] And that same effect is felt by teachers, especially after years of the same topic (or versions of it). Taking information and transforming it can have as much an effect on the maker as it does on the information. The other value is that this kind of modelling can help avoid the mess of poster paints and cut-and-paste Prezis that inquiry- and project-based learning can fall into.

There are several ways you can make this content, but, if you are using the internet for basically anything, you will have noticed a sustained reliance on video as a tool to communicate messages.[6] But everyone knows this – everyone knows they should be making video content. It's just that it's so complicated. Creating a video at a school can be broken down into seven easy steps:

1. Find a camera at your school that 'works'; this is sometimes a relative term around schools. There will often be poorly organised cupboards bursting with VHS and MiniDV cameras and tapes – none of which will connect to a computer manufactured after 2008. Haranguing the Art/Media department can work well here or, in some cases, the library will have a state-of-the art recording set-up that no-one seems to have ever thought to inform the staff about.
2. Once you've got a camera in hand, film whatever it is you need.

3. Get the footage from the camera to your computer – this is where things get tricky and where 50 per cent of these projects fall off the rails. Ask someone for help. Search out the manual in aforementioned poorly organised cupboard. Post on a forum. Have a nervous breakdown. Search for a YouTube tutorial. Find a searchable PDF copy of the manual.
4. If you've managed to get the footage onto your computer, this is where the next roadblock comes in. You've resolved not to use Windows Movie Maker. Something more professional this time, you tell yourself. But these programs ask so many questions before you even get started. What resolution is a good resolution? What the hell is a 'scratch disk'?!
5. If you've got to this stage and you've got a project started (which puts you with about 5 per cent of users at this point), you begin to notice that you have a lot choices. Like, *a lot* of choices, and each one has a more confusing name than the last. And if you right-click, you double your choices. Some don't even have names, just symbols. And all your footage looks terrible. It's basically just out-of-focus shots on a fingerprint-smudged lens with the accompanying soundtrack of wind blowing directly into a microphone. Stanley Kubrick, eat your heart out.
6. This is where you look at the time and find you have spent six hours on this project with absolutely nothing to show. Cry a little. Give up.
7. Update original PowerPoint presentation.

Whether you gave up at Step 1 or made it all the way though to giving up at Step 6, one thing is true: it's really hard to make anything more than the film equivalent of a flaming pile of garbage. Smash cut to reveal … information already given away by this article's title: Adobe Premiere Clip. The easier way is Adobe Premiere Clip.

WHAT IS IT?

Premiere Clip is the mobile and tablet version of Adobe's flagship video-editing program, Premiere Pro. Adobe has been pushing Premiere Pro for years – improvements and tweaks have had the company slowly edging out competition through

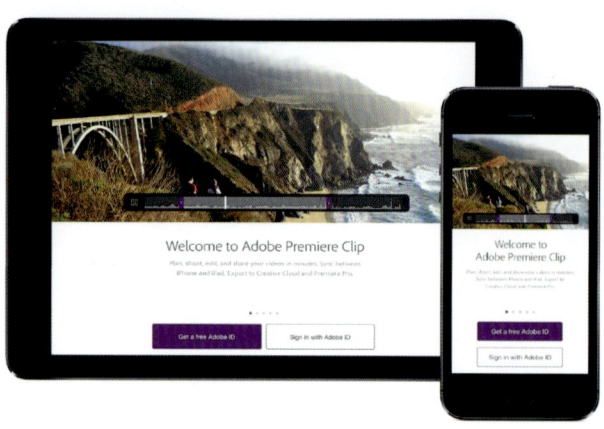

HOW DOES IT WORK?

Premiere Clip is great for that chasm that exists in education between expectation and reality. This chasm features some of the greatest hits of educational expectation: the assumption that today's teachers are digitally literate (with an even higher expectation for younger teachers); the assumption that these teachers can get their hands on the equipment and software they need (without incurring any extra cost to the school); the assumption that, due to the over-saturation of video in web and social media today, higher production values are much easier to attain; and the assumption that teachers have boundless free time in which to prepare these materials (maybe in their January 'lesson planning' time[9]). You can use Premiere Clip to edit videos and photographs on your phone – you can even utilise files from connected accounts (like Dropbox, Creative Cloud, etc.), which means you can incorporate content from multiple sources. It's a simple mobile editing interface that allows you to trim clips, adjust levels, reorder, insert titles, and add included royalty-free music. If that's too much, you can even set it to do an automatic edit – with this setting, Premiere Clip will cut your clips to the beat of one of the included musical pieces (which are packaged as Premiere Clip themes). Exporting (the bane of the beginning editor's existence) is similarly straightforward while also including a plethora of options. You can go the easy route and save straight back onto your device (or to one of your connected accounts), save to a connected YouTube or Twitter, send to

Premiere Clip takes all the good parts about your smartphone (portability, availability, great camera, great mic, powerful processor), as well as your comfort with it as a device, and turns it into a film-production unit.

making it easier to integrate across applications, making for a more efficient and cost-effective workflow.[7] But Premiere Clip isn't Pro's little brother – Adobe's already got one of those in Premiere Elements, an entry-level editing program designed for beginners and students. Premiere Clip is all about on-the-go filmmaking and a user-friendly workflow. It's part of a movement from Adobe over the past few years to solidify itself as a player in the mobile market, as well as push the interconnected nature of its applications.[8] Premiere Clip, like the majority of these apps, is device-agnostic, so it works on Android and iOS smartphones and tablets. And, unlike Premiere Pro and Elements, Clip is free. Totally free. Like the other Adobe mobile apps and services, all you need is an Adobe ID to use it.

Premiere Pro CC (if you have it) for further editing, or upload the video to Adobe's own server for hosting and sharing.

Premiere Clip takes all the good parts about your smartphone (portability, availability, great camera, great mic, powerful processor), as well as your comfort with it as a device, and turns it into a film-production unit. If you've got a train ride after an excursion, you could pretty easily use the time to knock out an edit of a video of the day's adventures. If you know you are going to be absent, you can edit together a video introduction for your class instead of leaving it to the substitute (the dreaded substitute) to explain. With a little practice and forethought, you can have the entire production process for a two- or three-minute video (filming, editing and distributing) done in about thirty or thirty-five minutes.

ADOBE PREMIERE CLIP TUTORIAL

You'll find Premiere Clip in the stores for both Android and iOS devices. You can also link to them through <http://premiereclip.adobe.com>.

1. Once you have Premiere Clip on your device, you just need to SIGN IN using an Adobe ID – or, if you don't have one, SIGN UP. Adobe IDs are free, easy to set up and allow you access to a range of different Adobe products and services, as well as allowing you to sync your projects across your devices.

2. The landing page in Premiere Clip is your MY PROJECTS page. From here you can relaunch old projects, start new ones (by clicking the plus symbol) or edit your preferences (via the Premiere Clip symbol on the left). You can also explore the COMMUNITY tab, which features other users' public projects as well as your own projects in the PUBLISHED tab.

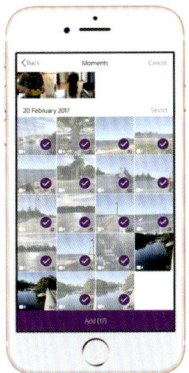

3. When you initiate a new project through the plus symbol, it asks you where you would like to source your footage from. You can choose to utilise footage from a Dropbox or Creative Cloud account, from Lightroom, from footage on your device, or you can take a new photo or video and create and edit your project on the move.

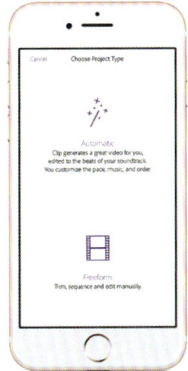

4. At the beginning of a project you have the option to choose either an Automatic or Freeform project type. Freeform projects give you a lot more control, but Automatic projects are quicker and utilise Clip's 'cut to the beat' functionality. As a rule of thumb, Automatic works great for projects that utilise photographs and Freeform works better for video.

5. With my Freeform project chosen, I have all my clips together in the project. The preview image of each clip also indicates the clip's run time and whether it is a video or photograph. Underneath the preview of the selected clip is a waveform representation of the clip's sound and two purple bookends that are used to trim the clip.

6. Clips that have been selected by mistake can be removed easily by selecting the X symbol in the corner and then the subsequent trash symbol. This just removes the clip from the project and has no effect on the location of the clip on the user's device.

7. Reordering (or sequencing) your videos is as simple as selecting them and dragging them around like an 8-puzzle with each preview block shifting to allow room. The simplest approach to editing is to sort out the sequencing of your clips before working through trimming clips down.

8. By changing the position of the purple bookends, you change what part of the clip will play as part of the project. Unlike other editing programs, you don't need to commit these edits. Premiere Clip simply plays back only the areas of the project within the purple bookends.

9. Selecting the speaker icon opens up the audio options for the clip you have selected. This footage was all taken at the waterfront so it is pretty windy – you can see from the peaks in the waveform that the wind was a big factor. As a result I'm going to turn the audio off for this clip (and do the same on all the other clips too).

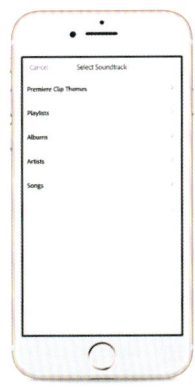

10. Selecting the music note icon will open up the SELECT SOUNDTRACK option. You do have the option to pick music from your device. But, while Ween's 'Buenas Tardes Amigo' might go really well with the footage I've put together, using music I don't have the rights to severely limits what I can do with this project. Luckily, the program comes packaged with PREMIERE CLIP THEMES.

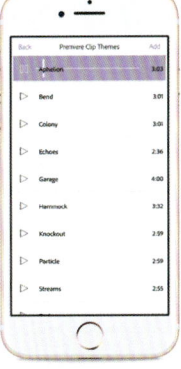

11. These themes are all royalty-free and yours to use in your project regardless of where your end product goes. You could even use these to make a commercial video to go on your school's website. There are ten tracks in total (or were, at the time of writing), and they cover a variety of styles and feels so there is sure to be a track here that will fit your project.

12. With your soundtrack selected, you have a few options, including when the music starts, VOLUME, AUTO MIX (which will dip the music when sound is louder in a clip – like when people are speaking) as well as the SYNC TO MUSIC feature, which can help to create a significantly slicker end product.

 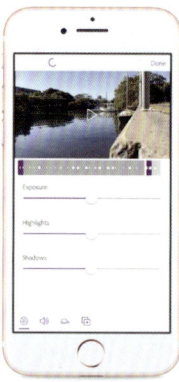 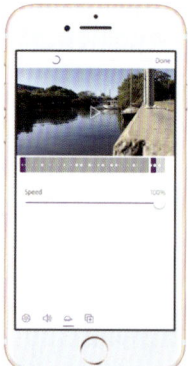 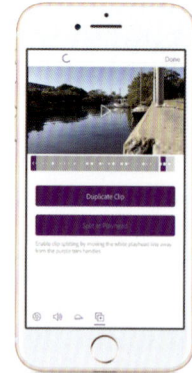

13. The SYNC TO MUSIC feature makes it easier to trim your clips to the beat of the music, giving you beat indicators and snapping your bookends to them. These beats are represented on the waveform track as circles – the size of the circle represents the prominence of the beat or a change in the music.

14. Selecting the shutter icon allows you to edit individual clip properties so that you can ensure that each clip looks its best and fits in with the rest of the production. You are able to adjust the overall EXPOSURE as well as HIGHLIGHTS and SHADOWS using simple sliders.

15. The turtle symbol represents the speed of the clip, which you can adjust to suit the kind of feel you are trying to establish. At present the highest speed level in Premiere Clip is 100 per cent (which means there is no ability to speed up a clip), but this is a feature that has been raised on a range of Adobe forums so it is certainly possible that it could change in the future.

16. You also have the option to duplicate a clip (which can be useful for using clips in different places within a project) or to split a clip at the playhead. This involves playing the clip through to the point you want to separate the clip in two, and then selecting this option. This can be useful for longer clips with numerous pieces of useful content.

 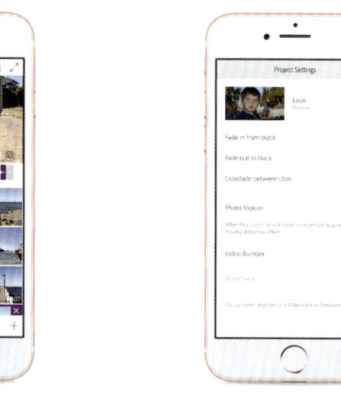

17. There is also the ability to add more footage as you go – the options remain the same as they were at project creation. You can add titles to your production, too, which can help with a professional feel but can also be useful for any explanations you might need.

18. While the titles you can add are quite simple (a choice of two colours, no ability to change font type or size, and no ability to have a title over video), they still add a great finishing touch to a production. You can also utilise the titles as storycards, which can be used as placeholders for footage you haven't yet filmed.

19. Once your title has been created, it operates the same as any other asset in Premiere Clip – it can be moved around by being selected and dragged, and its time can be changed through adjustments to its bookends. You can insert as many titles as you like into a project.

20. The cog icon represents the PROJECT SETTINGS. These include things like FADE IN FROM BLACK and FADE OUT FROM BLACK, CROSSFADE BETWEEN CLIPS (sometimes known as a 'dissolve'), the option of a WATERMARK, the option of a VIDEO BUMPER (sometimes known as a 'stinger' – a piece of footage that plays after the product, usually a representation of a production company), as well as a range of LOOKS.

 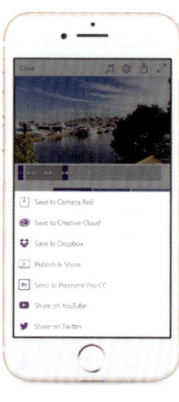  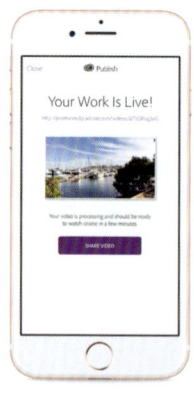

21. The Premiere Clip LOOKS are a range of programmed filters that enable you to establish an aesthetic across all of your clips at once (which can help in tying everything together and making it appear more professional). As you select each effect, you will see your footage change to show the effect in action.

22. When you are satisfied with your project, you can export it. You have a range of options for sharing your end product. The option to SEND TO PREMIERE PRO CC allows users with Adobe Creative Cloud memberships to start a project on their mobile device and then send it over to their computer for fine-tuning and finishing (without the need for heaps of cables and connections).

23. Selecting PUBLISH & SHARE will let you share your video on the Adobe Premiere Clip server (like an Adobe YouTube). You have the option to share your project publicly so that others can find it, or make it unlisted. An unlisted project is easily accessible to those with the link, but it isn't able to be searched for by other users.

24. After a little processing, your work will be live and ready to share. Selecting SHARE VIDEO will open up your sharing options, which include all the usual suspects – email, SMS, Facebook, Twitter, and copy link.

The video I created is available at <http://premiereclip.adobe.com/videos/J2TzDFug3xG>.

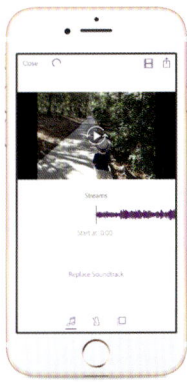    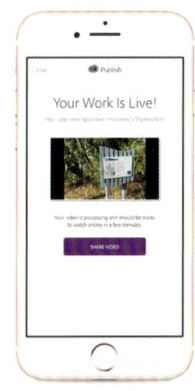

25. While there is a lot of freedom in the Freeform approach, there are many projects that will perfectly suit the Automatic project type – anything that is predominantly photographic will work well. You start an Automatic project the same way as a Freeform one, but from there your options are limited to SOUNDTRACK, PACING and SEQUENCING.

26. Automatic projects work better the more content you have. Around forty-five to sixty photographs can get you a pretty reasonable end product – Automatic projects are cut to the beat so they can move quite quickly through your content. You do have the option to adjust your pacing (and as you do you will notice the overall duration will change). I tend to utilise the second-slowest option the most.

27. The sequencing option works exactly the same here as it does in Freeform. It's just a matter of dragging your clips around to where you want them to be and then playing them to see how they look. The other thing you may notice in a project is that your photographs have black bars on the edges. This is because they are taken at a different ratio. The same will be true of photos or videos in other formats (especially if you are the sort of animal who records in portrait format).

28. You can use an Automatic project as a starting point and convert it into a Freeform project. This can work well as an easy way to get a project underway. Unfortunately, you can't go the other way, though – once you have converted it, the only way back is to start again.

29. Automatic has the same share options as Freeform.

    The video I created is available at <http://premiereclip.adobe.com/videos/VThp4mvN3fe>.

    It's a really solid editing platform that is very useful and fun to use. A great way to give your ideas some oomph.

Kevin Lavery was an Art and Media teacher in Melbourne for nearly ten years before packing up for life in Brisbane. He is now the Training & Liaison Officer for TAFE Queensland's eLearning Services. Kevin regularly presents as part of the free online Adobe Generation professional learning courses and webinars. In his spare time he undertakes 'art projects'; the latest is an Ishihara test self-portrait. See this and 100 other self-portraits on his @KevLavery Instagram account. **SE**

Endnotes

[1] Marc Prensky, 'Digital Natives, Digital Immigrants', *On the Horizon*, vol. 9, no. 5, October 2001, pp. 1–6.

[2] David Lightman is a character played by Matthew Broderick in the film *WarGames* (John Badham, 1983).

[3] See Sue Bennett et al., 'The "Digital Natives" Debate: A Critical Review of the Evidence', *British Journal of Educational Technology*, vol. 39, no. 5, pp. 775–86.

[4] Brendan Casey, 'Allen's Lollies Accused of a Lack of Variety in Their Party Mix Packets', *Herald Sun*, 17 December 2013, <http://www.heraldsun.com.au/news/allens-lollies-accused-of-a-lack-of-variety-in-their-party-mix-packets/news-story/f0932e83d73076faae48b0a1ab3083e7>, accessed 19 April 2017.

[5] Stephanie Bell, 'Project-based Learning for the 21st Century: Skills for the Future', *The Clearing House: A Journal of Educational Strategies, Issues and Ideas*, vol. 83, no. 2, 2010, pp. 39–43.

[6] *The State of Video Marketing*, Demand Metric, November 2016, <http://awesome.vidyard.com/rs/273-EQL-130/images/State%20of%20Video%20Marketing%20-%20Nov%202016%20-%20Benchmark%20Report.pdf>, accessed 19 April 2017.

[7] Robert Hardy, 'How an All-Adobe Workflow Made the Post Production of *Gone Girl* Insanely Efficient', *No Film School*, 10 October 2014, <http://nofilmschool.com/2014/10/how-all-adobe-workflow-made-post-production-gone-girl-insanely-efficient>, accessed 19 April 2017.

[8] Have a look at the whole suite of mobile apps at <http://www.adobe.com/au/creativecloud/catalog/mobile.html>, accessed 19 April 2017.

[9] See AAP, 'Queensland Andrew Laming Takes Aim at School Teachers on Facebook', *The Courier Mail*, 11 January 2017, <http://www.couriermail.com.au/news/queensland/queensland-andrew-laming-takes-aim-at-school-teachers-on-facebook/news-story/b3cdb7573d10015a8be38ab7425dbb05>, accessed 19 April 2017.

VIRTUAL TOOLKIT

BLOXELS
http://www.bloxelsbuilder.com
Cost: US$49.95 (starter kit)
from US$250 (classroom packs)

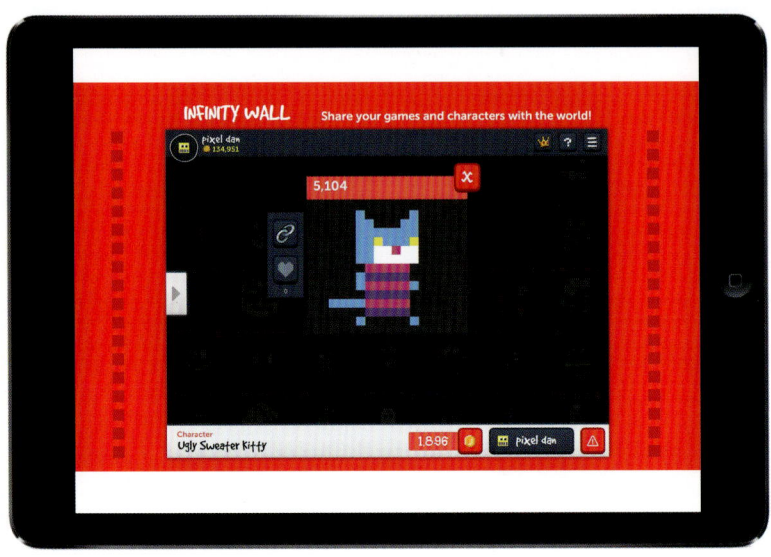

There are a number of great game-making and gameplay resources out there for you to utilise in your classroom, but Bloxels is the first of its kind: it brings physical block designs to life in the digital world. The Bloxels Video Game Builder Starter Kit contains the blocks, the gameboard, a challenge poster and a guidebook, while the Bloxels Classroom Packs are a cost-effective way to purchase multiple kits. The Bloxels Builder app – which is free to download as part of either purchasing option – is available for download on iOS, Android and Kindle devices.

The STEAM-focused learning principles encompassed by this unique resource certainly make it full of great contemporary educational opportunities. After creating their coloured block designs on the gameboard, students can 'transport' these into the app and watch them magically 'transform' into digitised videogame levels decked out with terrain, water, lava, power-ups, coins, enemies and hazards to avoid, as well as a number of other stationary and moving objects. Characters, terrains, game layouts and game objects are created by placing the colour-coded blocks onto the square gameboard. To convert this physical design into a digital format, students use their device's camera; they need to ensure all corners of the gameboard are visible in the frame, and it seems to work best if the gameboard is on a white background and free of any glare. The tutorial videos on the Bloxels website offer fantastic assistance for first-time users, helping to build students' confidence and sense of preparedness.

Once they've captured the gameboard designs, students can test each level and iron out any issues with the original design, all of which can be implemented on the digital representation of their level using the app's CONFIGURE function. From here, students can add characters, animations (like enemies to destroy), background and mid-ground designs, as well as board designs that are stamped over the static block colours, giving them texture and life. Textual information can also be included to add a storytelling aspect to the game.

During the design process, students have lots to consider to ensure they lay out workable and exciting floors/levels. The methodology of design thinking will be in full swing as students are challenged to understand and develop creative ways to solve specific issues, make predictions, test theories and make revisions. Beyond design thinking, Bloxels teaches students STEAM-focused learning principles like prototyping, teamwork, collaboration and user empathy.

The final steps when making games using Bloxels are 'play' and 'share', which do require users to create an account. When a game is ready to share, students can publish it to Bloxels' Infinity Wall and earn coins when others play their game. The Infinity Wall allows students to explore the games made by other creators, and gather ideas for their own designs. They can also use any coins earned to buy content from other games, which can be customised into their own games, promoting the continual evolution of game design and gameplay.

Bloxels has created a few complementary resources to support teachers, but the instructions, challenges and worksheets will need to be adapted to suit your students' age and abilities, your classroom's size and school's resources. You can choose either the one-day or five-day curriculum lesson plan and activities, which are built around the design-thinking process. Both options include a lesson plan summary, objectives, instructions, design challenge, brainstorming worksheet and assessment questions. The five-day lesson plan also includes a marking rubric.

> The STEAM-focused learning principles encompassed by this unique resource certainly make it full of great contemporary educational opportunities.

JANE SHIELDS surveys digital resources for teachers and their classrooms.

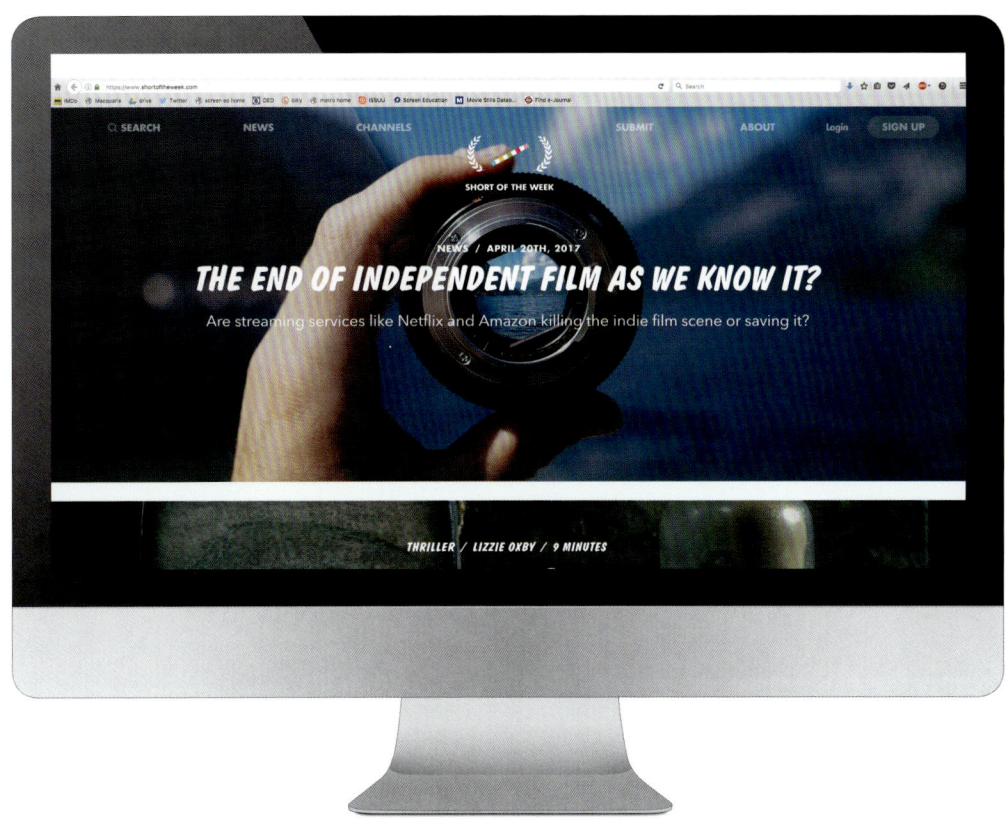

Short of the Week not only allows teachers and students to engage with the work of emerging filmmakers, but also provides an inexpensive avenue for student filmmakers to gain exposure for their original work.

SHORT OF THE WEEK
http://www.shortoftheweek.com
Cost: free

Short of the Week brings together a range of original, creative, entertaining and technically proficient short films, as well as informative articles on navigating film festivals and interviews with shorts directors. While not all of the short films featured on the site are suitable for classroom viewing, a large number of them – particularly in light of their format – are perfect for the classroom setting. The shorts vary in genre, and their shorter timeframe suits the sporadic attention span of many young people.

The website's clean and easy-to-use layout is another drawcard for teachers and students. Every week, the homepage spotlights a diverse number of great short films, or you can go straight to the CHANNELS tab, where the films are categorised by 'Genre', 'Topic', 'Style', 'Collections' or 'Country'. The 'Collections' option includes a number of great playlists that group together films that are contest winners, featured in festivals like Tribeca and Sundance, student-made, family-friendly, made with super 16mm or DSLR, by female filmmakers, or take the form of web series.

Short of the Week not only allows teachers and students to engage with the work of emerging filmmakers, but also provides an inexpensive (there is a US$29 submission fee) avenue for student filmmakers to gain exposure for their original work and make connections with top industry influencers. The Short of the Week team is made up of the industry's top short-film curators, and through the site, students can access resources to help them workshop their ideas, get feedback and get noticed.

FRANKIE MAGAZINE FOR SCHOOLS

http://www.frankie.com.au/schools
Cost: free

Publisher frankie press is known for its smart, eclectic and witty magazines and books. Regular readers may have already identified many teaching and learning opportunities that can be linked to the contents of its print products, but now, frankie has developed a specific collection of teaching resources for high schools that align nicely with the Australian Curriculum for Media Arts and English. frankie magazine for Schools is a set of comprehension, analysis and writing activities with a very flexible approach. The activities can be specifically aligned to issues of frankie, or you can modify the activities to suit other magazines or stimulus material.

While the activities are originally designed for Years 9 and 10 English and Media Arts classes as well as VCE English Unit 1 and VCE Media Unit 2, there is room for these resources to be adapted to suit other curriculum areas, such as Visual Arts, Digital Technologies, and Work Studies. Whatever the subject area, the activities share a common focus: encouraging and developing students' abilities to think critically and creatively while also developing their ICT skills.

Teachers should start by downloading the 'Ideas and Activities for Using frankie magazine in the Classroom' PDF, which gives an INTRO, OUTLINE and METHOD for each classroom activity. Students will be looking at language, content, style and themes, and are guided through a variety of tasks including research, brainstorm, analysis, creation and reflection tasks. For example, the 'Everybody Has a Story' activity looks at the content and style of autobiographical or biographical nonfiction articles published in frankie magazine. These personal stories are really engaging, inspirational stimuli that students can use to analyse text structure, organisation, tone and themes. They can then research and write their own article after brainstorming with a peer, interviewing, writing, reviewing, editing and redrafting. You can even collate these stories into a class blog or a similar platform for sharing and celebrating student work.

All the frankie examples referred to in the PDF are available for free from the frankie website, and Australian teachers, librarians and students can also avail of a 25 per cent discount when taking up a frankie subscription.

> frankie magazine for Schools is a set of comprehension, analysis and writing activities with a very flexible approach. The activities can be specifically aligned to issues of frankie, or you can modify the activities to suit other magazines or stimulus material.

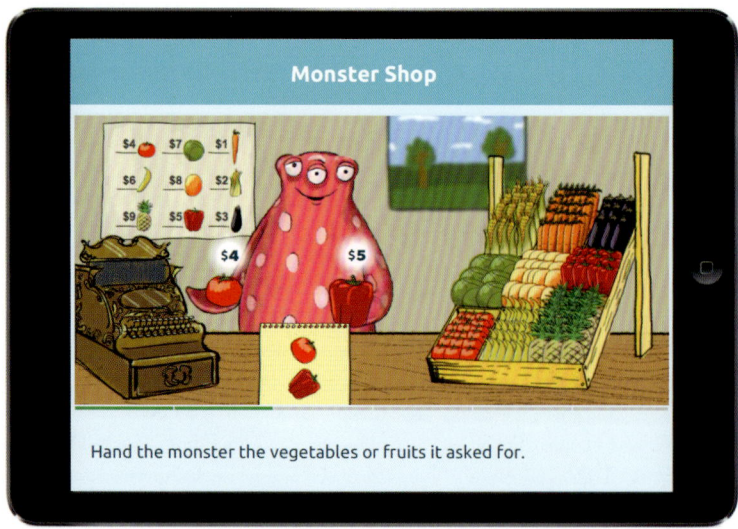

MATIFIC

http://www.matific.com
Cost: free (thirty-day trial)
from A$12 per year (subscription)

Matific aims to help kids tackle the growing issue of maths anxiety by immersing them in an interactive and fun adaptation of your typical classroom Maths lesson. Matific episodes comprise game-orientated tasks, from five to fifteen minutes in length, exploring a specific mathematical insight, concept or skill in real-world scenarios, making them more relatable for students and easier to understand.

Available on the website or via the iOS or Android app, the tasks are designed for students in Foundation through to Year 6, with a wide variety of activities and worksheets aligned with the Australian Curriculum. Topics range from counting and identifying 2D and 3D shapes at the Foundation level, through to algebraic thinking, statistics, measurement conversions and financial mathematics in Year 6.

LITTLE LUNCH APP

http://actf.com.au/education-programs/little-lunch-app

Cost: free

The *Little Lunch* App gives students the opportunity to create, develop and share their own short stories that mirror the format of episodes from the award-winning ABC3 TV show *Little Lunch*. This Australian series documents life in a primary school playground through clever, humorous and appealing fifteen-minute-long episodes. The app, which developed out of this premise, gives students a unique cross-media experience with which they can create

> The app … gives students a unique cross-media experience with which they can create a personalised episode using the same conventions, procedures and narrative structure as the TV series.

a personalised episode using the same conventions, procedures and narrative structure as the TV series.

The app is available for download on both Android and iOS platforms, and guides students through a two-stage creation process. Stage 1 steps through establishing the 'who' and 'where' components of the episode, while the more elaborate Stage 2 is concerned with the creation of the story arc, time and narrative structure, as well as audio components. During Stage 2, students film five scenes that will make up their short story; they can set these scenes in either the past or the present, and they can utilise natural sounds from each setting or add a voiceover. *Little Lunch* App stories don't need to be complex; in fact, the simplicity of the TV series is one aspect that makes it so distinctive and engaging. The aim is to utilise this app to help primary school students understand the basic structure and principles of storytelling while encouraging them to be creative and come up with original ideas.

After completing both stages, students can witness their personalised content transform into a short film. Their productions can be uploaded and shared online, or simply saved to the Android or iOS device. Also available is a helpful teacher's guide, which identifies relevant curriculum links for both the TV series and the app. It likewise covers each stage of the app's production process, offers additional activity ideas that enhance students' storytelling knowledge and techniques, and includes a synopsis for all existing *Little Lunch* episodes.

. . . .

Matific is well organised and easy to navigate, so it shouldn't take long for even the youngest students to learn how to interact with the platform. The resources are organised by year level and topic, and although some areas contain fewer resources than others, what is great to see is a continuation of some topics across year levels, with increasing increments of challenge and conceptual understanding. This is perfect for testing and tracking students' development in fundamental maths skills across a number of years. The TEACHER DASHBOARD option also makes it simple to monitor and share student progress. The dashboard is easy to set up, and diagnostic data such as progress reports can be emailed directly to teachers and parents.

Research into the academic benefits of Matific revealed that it can help 'improve students' maths test results by 34%', and I think the trial-and-error method used in the games is somewhat responsible for these results. It's a positive method for encouraging students to have another go, and less threatening for students who experience maths anxiety. Each activity allows students to try a few times to find a correct solution before Matific reveals the answer to them. Some of the tasks even have more than one correct solution, which accommodates students' differing approaches to problem-solving while also presenting different ways to think about a mathematical concept.

The free 30-day trial is a great opportunity for you to have a go at using Matific in the classroom as part of your existing lessons and activities. Once you have identified the episodes relevant to your classes, the ACTIVITY feature allows you to easily assign specific tasks to the entire class or individual students. The games can act as opening stimuli for concepts covered in existing Maths textbooks or lessons, or they can be used after introducing the concepts as a means of enhancing understanding

> Matific is well organised and easy to navigate, so it shouldn't take long for even the youngest students to learn how to interact with the platform.

and as formative assessment. There are a range of valuable supporting resources such as written teacher guides, video guides, talks, lesson plans and user tutorials. The teacher guides are particularly thorough and help connect the use of Matific episodes to classroom lessons; most of the guides provide a DESCRIPTION; a BEHIND THE SCENE overview, which covers information such as activity objectives and learning intentions, as well as hints on how to interact with the activity; PRESENTATION instructions; DISCUSSION prompts; and specific ACTIVITIES. **SE**

Best in the West

Genre, John Wayne and the American Dream in John Ford's *The Searchers*

BRIAN MCFARLANE

John Ford's *The Searchers* (1956) is so rich a film that it is hard to know where to start – or what to include and what to omit, given that this study is of finite length. Some of the matters that seem crucial to consider include: the western as a genre; Ford as perhaps its most famous exponent; the star persona of John Wayne, protagonist of Ford's and other directors' westerns; the film's narrative patterns; and its ideological content in relation to the times of its setting and of its production. It won't be possible to cover all these aspects of the film in detail, but, in thinking further about it, they are all indispensable.

GENRE AND THE WESTERN

Not all films of course fit snugly into this or that genre, but the idea of genre as a loose set of conventions has helped to categorise productions as, say, musicals, thrillers, romantic comedies – or westerns. It is not a matter of rules, but of conventions that have become recognisable through much use, though one must always be open to variations on these.[1]

The western is one of the most enduring genres, dating from the silent-film days, though tapering off in recent decades, and is often characterised by recurring thematic and narrative interests. These can include pioneering difficulties in the face of daunting landscapes or hostile American Indians, or a stranger coming into a threatened community, or the conflict of small farmers against cattle barons, or the growth of civilisation against forces of lawlessness. There are narrative subsets such as the classic western

(hero entering community, dealing with villains, becoming part of the society he has protected, etc.) or the vengeance western, or even the odd musical western and the spaghetti western (of course, from Italy). What is often a major source of interest is how the film deals with – reworks – a sense of what the west was like as a place of human interaction with its dangers and challenges. And a further interest often lies in the way the western is made to resonate with American life at the time of a film's production.

In terms of iconography, of the recognisable *look* of things, one thinks of such matters as settings, costume and certain star presences. Often there will be a little town with a single street

It is a John Ford film and it stars John Wayne, and these two names are both potent in any study of the western – and nowhere more significantly than in *The Searchers*.

dwarfed by a vast landscape, or a setting even more isolated, as in *The Searchers*, which has a sole cabin in what seems a daunting emptiness, or the main setting may be a military outpost. As to costume, we expect the men to be in dungarees and checked shirts, and the women, in simple gingham dignity unless they are saloon girls who will be more adventurously (that is, skimpily) dressed. Some star presences, almost entirely male, became part of the iconography of the genre: actors such as Randolph Scott, Joel McCrea, Roy Rogers, for a while Clint Eastwood and perhaps above all John Wayne served to define the look of the western, almost to the point where it was hard to accept them in a business suit in other films.

Mention of the look of the western reminds me that we should also be aware of how the films' *sound* is so often a key element in their generic texture. Some famous Hollywood composers wrote music specially for particular films, and there was also a tendency to draw on folk music or popular ballads and hymn tunes to call up the historical past that was the period setting for most westerns.

The above may seem like a skirmishing approach to the film at issue in this study, but no film is made in a vacuum and there are several contexts in which *The Searchers* needs to be considered. Its genre is perhaps the most obvious, but it is also a John Ford film and it stars John Wayne, and these two names are both potent in any study of the western – and nowhere more significantly than in *The Searchers*.

THE WESTERN AND TWO KEY NAMES

John Ford

At a controversial Hollywood meeting of the Screen Directors Guild in October 1950, Ford announced himself thus: 'My name is John Ford. I am a director of Westerns'.[2] This prompted some laughter, presumably because Ford's name was so indissolubly associated with the genre. He made some famous films in other modes and genres, including *The Grapes of Wrath* (1940), a poetic study of a community forced to keep moving for survival, the mining drama *How Green Was My Valley* (1941), and the Irish-set romance *The Quiet Man* (1952), but in genre terms the westerns outnumbered the others. His *Stagecoach* (1939) brought new distinction to the genre and enacted a characteristic Fordian theme: that of testing human qualities under stress. *My Darling Clementine* (1946) celebrates the growth of a civilised community in the face of lawlessness; *Fort Apache* (1948), *She Wore a Yellow Ribbon* (1949) and *Rio Grande* (1950) form a loose 'Cavalry trilogy', offering studies of institutional life (that is, of the military), of the interaction of the individual with that institution, of the rewards of such a life, and of women's roles in such a male milieu; and *The Man Who Shot Liberty Valance* (1962) is, at least in part, a melancholy elegy for the west as a spent force.

All of these films have abundant rewards for the viewer, but I would claim that *The Searchers*, grimmer, darker, more complex and ambiguous than any of the others, is Ford's indisputable masterpiece. Other directors, such as Howard Hawks, made fine westerns and Ford made other sorts of films, but no-one else has been more powerfully and insistently associated with the genre.

John Wayne

The star in any film is likely to be a key signifier in the texture of its meaning, as a result of the combination of physical attributes and persona established over films in which he/she has performed. In 1956, the year of *The Searchers*, Wayne's name was primarily associated with westerns, though there had also been some popular war films (including Ford's *They Were Expendable*, 1945), and the odd romantic drama (such as *Reunion in France*, Jules Dassin, 1942) and comedy (see *Without Reservations*, Mervyn LeRoy, 1946). He had also appeared in westerns for other directors and would go on to act in three major ones for Howard Hawks – *Rio Bravo* (1959), *El Dorado* (1967) and *Rio Lobo* (1970) – but it is with Ford his persona and, indeed, his career and name are most tenaciously associated.

His role in Ford's *Stagecoach* was the turning point in a career in which he would become the archetypal US star, even for those who would have disdained his extremely conservative political and social views. He was characteristically presented as the tough, laconic western hero: tall, solidly built, physically courageous, sometimes brutal, his attitude to women a mix of treat-'em-rough and chivalrous. In fact though, he has given more complex performances than this persona might suggest, in films such as Hawks' *Red River* (1948), Ford's *She Wore a Yellow Ribbon* and, above all, *The Searchers*, in which there is rarely a moment when he is not suggesting a complicated life beneath the rugged masculine surface. And just once, in the first version of *True Grit* (Henry Hathaway, 1969), there is an engaging element of self-parody; for instance, when he says of the spirited girl who wants to engage him for a venture, 'She reminds me of me.'

THE SEARCHERS AS A FILM OF TWO JOHNS

So, given the range of conventions that help to define the western as a genre, and the expectations the names of Ford and Wayne tend to conjure up, just how do these surface in this richly textured example of their work in the genre with which the two are so closely associated? It will be helpful to have this in mind as we turn to look in detail at the film, since these two constitute such crucial aspects of the film's context.

The Searchers deals with some of the characteristic oppositions of Ford's westerns, and indeed of the genre at large. These include the contrasts of the loner and the community, of civilisation and the wilderness. There is rough comedy (as in 'funny fights') and powerful emotion. As one commentary on Ford has it: 'In his greatest works, the plot line oscillates freely between the tragic and the ridiculous',[3] or to put it more bluntly, paraphrasing a critic whose name I can't recall, the breadth of the comedy is the price that we pay for the depth of the feeling in a Ford film. When two young men brawl in an episode near the end of *The Searchers*, we – and the bystanders in the scene, including the putative bride of one of them – are encouraged to view the stoush as comic. Then, not ten minutes later, we will be confronted with film's most heart-stopping moment (more on that shortly).

Then there is that awesome (in the serious meaning of that word) use of natural setting, in which rudimentary houses have an exposed look, as if unprotected from any threat the landscape might throw up, let alone from dangerous human elements. In this matter, we also see the Ford who is fascinated by the historical origins that underpin the narrative impulses of his films. Here, the idea of a white woman taken away by marauding Indians who have killed and/or raped her family members and destroyed her home offers a view of the dangers of western life in 1868, albeit espousing an illiberal view of the Indian way of living. In 2013, Glenn Frankel's book *The Searchers: The Making of an American Legend* chronicled the real-life account of Cynthia Ann Parker, who was kidnapped by Comanches, was raised by the tribe and was only restored to her white family twenty-four years later.[4] On this historical incident is Ford's film based, just as Alan Le May's 1954 novel, *The Searchers*, had been.

Among Ford's westerns, *The Searchers* was not particularly well-received at the time of its release, but it now enjoys classic status with critics and is venerated by other filmmakers. These include Paul Schrader, Martin Scorsese and Steven Spielberg, all of whom made films critics claimed were influenced by it[5] – and even the opening sequence of *Star Wars* (George Lucas, 1977) strongly evokes the scene in which Martin (Jeffrey Hunter) returns home to find his family has been slaughtered by Indians. As long ago as 1979, a newspaper article asserted that 'all recent American cinema derives from John Ford's *The Searchers*'.[6]

The idea of a white woman taken away by marauding Indians who have killed and/or raped her family members and destroyed her home offers a view of the dangers of western life in 1868, albeit espousing an illiberal view of the Indian way of living.

The character of Ethan Edwards, as played by Wayne, meets many of the expectations of his star persona. Ethan is strong, independent, laconic, adventurous and sometimes brutal. However, Ethan is made more complex as Wayne registers his unspoken love for his sister-in-law Martha (Dorothy Jordan), by the inherent racism of his hatred of Indians, by the solitariness that denotes him as belonging nowhere, and by his obsession with the girl who is the goal of his search. Wayne makes of Ethan a very unusual western hero, and it will be worth having in mind these two men – and the kinds of images of their work that they inevitably bring with them – in any close study of the film.

TWO FORERUNNERS

I've referred to Frankel's book, which so absorbingly chronicles the historical background story. The central thread that weaves its way through the book's first half involves the abduction of Parker. She was born into a pioneering family that dug itself into Texas in the 1830s, aiming at, but not always achieving, peaceful coexistence with its Mexican neighbours – or with the Indian population, which viewed 'Parker's Fort' as a military installation, and therefore fair game. Following an Indian raid, the young girl is taken by the Comanche, and lives with them for two decades, during which she bears three children. Her uncle, James Parker, prototype for the Ethan Edwards character of the film, institutes a search for her, but, unlike Ethan, gives up on the search, partly for health reasons, partly because he's repelled by the idea of her having been wife or concubine to a Comanche warrior. All this is seen against, and as part of, the sweep of US history, taking in the appropriation of land, the appalling conflict between races, the horror of civil war, and the confidence in white civilisation's right to impose its religious views and technological advance on the 'barbarous indigenes'.

Alan Le May's novel, on which the film is based,[7] sets the story of the Edwards family in Texas 1868 and he chooses to focus – as his title suggests – not on the victim or the captors, but on the men who search for the missing girls. He finds admiration for strong female characters in a world dominated by often-violent men, and he also finds sympathy for the Indian cause. His novel opens as the film does in establishing a kind of domesticity that will be threatened. Wayne's biographer records that Frank Nugent's screenplay 'made a full roster of changes' to the novel: for instance, in Le May's text, 'the kidnapped Debbie falls in love with Marty', and the Ethan character (Amos in the book) dies in the end.[8] I haven't space to go into the book at length, but one small detail has stayed with me: Nugent changed the name of the neighbouring family from Mathieson to Jorgensen, the Scandinavian origins of whom add another strand to the film's evocation of a multicultural America.

HOW THE FILM WORKS

Narrative pattern

1. THE OUTSIDER ARRIVES. The name 'Ethan' is the first word spoken in the film, and the way has been prepared by the title song (by Stan Jones) that accompanies the credits, the opening line of which is 'What makes a man to wander?

2. THE COMMUNITY IS ATTACKED. Rev. Sam Clayton (Ward Bond), part parson, part Texas Ranger, arrives with news of Comanche maraudings, involving the theft of the Jorgensens' cattle, and swears in Aaron and nephew Martin, who is one-eighth Indian. Ethan insists that Aaron not ride off with Clayton on some punitive expedition, and volunteers himself.

3. THE SEARCH BEGINS. Aaron and Martha's two daughters are found to have been kidnapped by the Comanche; the older girl, Lucy (Pippa Scott), is later found murdered and by implication raped, while we have seen the Indian chief Scar (Henry Brandon) standing in a threatening pose over the little girl, Debbie (Lana Wood), who has been sent to hide in a graveyard. Ethan, joined by the determined Marty, commits to the search for Debbie, and the centre of the film records the events of this five-year trek through hazardous territories and changing seasons.

4. THE FINDING. Five years later, they find her in an Indian settlement, which she now believes is her true home. Ethan, with his instinctive racism, tries to kill her, because she has become 'the leavin's of a Comanche buck', but is felled by an arrow from Scar. A short time after, an early morning raid on the Indian village leads to Ethan's killing Scar and to his pursuit of the fleeing Debbie (now played by *Natalie* Wood), and in the film's transcendent moment he picks her up and with Martin rides off to the Jorgensen homestead.

5. THE OUTSIDER REMAINS OUTSIDE. Mrs Jorgensen (Olive Carey) welcomes Debbie and leads her inside, followed by Martin and Laurie (Vera Miles), the Jorgensen daughter he loves, but the film's last shot is of Ethan seen alone outside.

Merely to note this overall structure is to give little idea of *The Searchers*' richness. It may be helpful to consider some of the film's use of parallelism on several levels.

Parallelism

1. PATTERNS OF EVENTS. The film is flanked by two returns: the first, when Ethan rides in to his brother's home; and the second, when he brings Debbie to the Jorgensens at the

There are several important parallels, for comparison or contrast, among the characters. A key one is that between Ethan and Scar as two dominant male figures, both capable of cruelty, both leaving much to be desired in their treatment of women.

What makes a man to roam?' The motif of the outsider who rides in is a common one, and not just in westerns, but it has rarely been achieved so movingly as here. It evokes questions from the outset: what is the basis for the somewhat strained greetings he receives? The ensuing scenes in his brother Aaron's (Walter Coy) cabin will lead us to ponder further, as he brusquely answers Aaron's queries and as an erotic tension seems hinted at between Ethan and Martha.

end. The first of these gives way to a departure, when the search gets underway; as to the latter, can we feel other than that Ethan will leave again? Why else would Ford choose to close the film with that shot, seen again through the doorway, of Ethan standing alone outside?

There are also essentially two searchers. The original search party has whittled down to just Ethan and Martin, but parallelism here gives way to contrast in their motives. Whereas Martin's whole aim is to bring little Debbie back to the settler's idea of home, Ethan's motive, after he has seen in an army outpost several women demented after abduction by Indians, is now to find and kill her.

In the two interrupted ceremonies – a funeral and a wedding – Ford almost insists on our seeing these as instances of civilisation making a stand in this harsh landscape by his use of the same hymn, 'Shall We Gather at the River?' The funeral – for Aaron and his family – comes to an end when Ethan strides off, impatient to be on the move, saying, 'Put an amen to it.' Mrs Jorgensen tries to restrain his obsessive urge to begin the search. The wedding, again involving Mrs Jorgensen's preparations, is to join Laurie, who has loved Marty but despaired of his return, and a dimly good-natured hayseed called Charlie McCorry (Ken Curtis). Marty and Ethan's return brings the ceremony to a halt and leads to a (comic) punch-up between Marty and Charlie.

2. IMAGES. Most obviously, the opening and closing images, as the vast landscape is viewed from the perspective of the open doorway of a homestead, reflect the use of such parallelism to make thematic issues emerge visually rather than spelling them out. Again, there are *two* homesteads, one of which has been destroyed, while the other survives, suggestive of the faltering progress of civilisation in the face of lawlessness and the wilderness. Though the film is concerned with the inroads of white progress, it does also allow the Indian encampment a certain look of orderliness. In all these images of home bases, it is less a matter of realism than of imagery used to distil ideas.

One of the most alarming moments in the film is that in which Scar stands threateningly above the child Debbie, and this image finds a parallel near the film's end when Ethan seems to occupy a similarly menacing stance over the fleeing Debbie. Ethan twice picks up Debbie. When he first returns to his brother's homestead, he lifts her playfully and affectionately, and, in the film's penultimate episode, after a breathtaking moment of suspense as we fear he may kill her, he finally lifts the grown girl with the words, 'Let's go home, Debbie.' In that image and in those words, so much of the film's complex meaning seems to fall into place.

3. CHARACTERS. There are several important parallels, for comparison or contrast, among the characters. A key one is that between Ethan and Scar as two dominant male figures, both capable of cruelty, both leaving much to be desired in their treatment of women. Speaking of women, think of Martha's tentative glances and gestures in relation to Ethan, and Laurie's franker approach to Marty; or of the two trios involving Ethan/Martha/Aaron and Marty/Lucy/Charlie and the different kinds of relationship structuring each; or of Martha and Mrs Jorgensen as two women who 'wouldn't let a man give up'. Most crucial of all are the emerging parallels between Ethan and Marty. In a sense, they are both outsiders, and Ford signals this early when each is given a solitary moment on the porch of the Edwards' home; they are both committed to the search, but their motivations are not the same; and in the end Marty is accepted into the Jorgensen home while Ethan remains symbolically outside.

These parallelisms are a crucial element in the film's structure, in its narrative action, in its images, and in accounting for its thematic richness. For instance, there is no clear-cut hero or villain: neither Ethan nor Scar qualifies for such a simplistic distinction. Nor does Marty's being received back into Laurie's arms and the Jorgensen home carry the same emotional weight as the ambiguity of Ethan's final image as outsider. Sometimes the parallels work for comparison, sometimes for contrasts, but they are always, at one level or other, telling us more about the lives that are the film's concern.

CONCLUSION

Frankel's book is subtitled 'The Making of an American Legend', and when one turns to the film, it has to be seen against, and part of, the sweep of US history. For example, there is the American romance of the opening up of the land: as Mrs Jorgensen says, 'Some day this is going to be a fine country to live in,' a remark that seems both to acknowledge the spirit of admirable enterprise that has been taming the wilderness and to imply that it will be a matter of keeping those Indians in check.

The film plainly contrasts adventurers and settlers; these are symbiotically dependent *and* incompatible. Settlers need Ethan but have no permanent place for him. The American dream is essentially a capitalist dream of a free-enterprise society, of ownership, sometimes at odds with the spirit that created it. Compare: Aaron's careful stashing away of money in the seat of a chair with Ethan's throwing the moneybag to him. Adaptability may be an element of this dream, epitomised in Rev. Clayton moving without question between the roles of clergyman and Texas Ranger captain.

Some years ago I ended a review[9] of Frankel's book with the comment that might equally apply to Ford's majestic cinematic reworking of it: 'This is the story of America.'

Brian McFarlane is an Adjunct Professor at Swinburne Institute of Technology and Adjunct Associate Professor at Monash University. His most recent books are Double-Act: The Remarkable Lives and Careers of Googie Withers and John McCallum *and* Twenty British Films: A Guided Tour. *His next is* The Afterlife of Brief Encounter. **SE**

Endnotes

1. For a useful discussion of the narrative conventions and structures of the genre, see Will Wright, *Six Guns and Society: A Structural Study of the Western*, University of California Press, Berkeley, 1975.
2. John Ford, quoted in Kevin Brianton, *Hollywood Divided: The 1950 Screen Directors Guild Meeting and the Impact of the Blacklist*, University Press of Kentucky, Lexington, 2016, p. 67.
3. Joseph McBride & Michael Wilmington, *John Ford*, Secker & Warburg, London, 1974, p. 32.
4. Glenn Frankel, *The Searchers: The Making of an American Legend*, Bloomsbury, New York, 2013.
5. For example, Scorsese's *Taxi Driver* (1976), Spielberg's *Close Encounters of the Third Kind* (1977) and Schrader's *Hardcore* (1979).
6. John L Hess & Peter Pringle, '*The Searchers*', *The Weekend Australian Magazine*, 11 March 1979, p. 6.
7. The film's screenplay credits read: 'Screenplay by Frank S. Nugent. From the novel by Alan Le May.'
8. Scott Eyman, *John Wayne: The Life and Legend*, Simon & Schuster, New York, 2014, p. 273.
9. Brian McFarlane, 'How the West Was Begun: Glenn Frankel's *The Searchers: The Making of an American Legend*', A2, *The Age*, 23 March 2013, p. 32, available at <http://www.theage.com.au/entertainment/books/how-the-west-was-begun-20130322-2gkrl.html>, accessed 28 March 2017.

'Hey, That's No Dame!'

Comedy and Performance in *Some Like It Hot*

ELOISE ROSS

Directed by German émigré Billy Wilder, *Some Like It Hot* (1959) is perhaps most distinctly memorable for its final line, 'Nobody's perfect.' Across his five-decade catalogue of work as a writer and director, Wilder is renowned for such punchlines, something that was likely learned from his mentor, fellow émigré Ernst Lubitsch. As a pithy response, the final line channels many themes of the film, most notably the acceptance of the role of performance in gender and identity. It could also be seen as a commentary on the structure of the film itself, which plays with genre and character conventions.

Some Like It Hot follows two musicians, Jerry (Jack Lemmon) and Joe (Tony Curtis), on the run after witnessing the Saint Valentine's Day Massacre in Chicago, who disguise themselves as women in an all-female band that tours to Miami. Set in 1929, the film is peppered with elements of the classic gangster genre, yet it is ultimately a lightning-paced comedic farce. Its first shot (after the raucous music of the opening credits) is one of sombre men surrounding a coffin in a hearse, and its first sound is a lonely siren in the distance. It is a dramatic scene, with the all-but-empty rain-trodden streets of Chicago illuminated by streetlamps and car headlights disrupted by screeching tires and a police chase. However, the mood soon changes. After a rain of gunfire, the camera pans down to focus on a steady stream of liquid leaking from bullet holes in the coffin, which clearly isn't blood. The men open it to reveal a stash of bootleg liquor, the liquid contents streaming from broken bottles. This is the Prohibition era, after all, and the men are gangsters. After this unexpected reveal, the plot simply moves on.

This opening scene is the first of several false starts, as the film returns at least once more to a serious modality, as though a straightforward gangster film. The next occurs when Detective Mulligan (Pat O'Brien) wanders into Mozzarella's Funeral Parlor and is let through another door inside, when the sombre

'Liebesträume' from the parlour organ transitions into the upbeat jazzy sound of 'Sweet Georgia Brown', wafting up from the stage of a lively speakeasy. When inside, planning a raid on the club, Mulligan leads with a line that jests with the bootleggers' grim cover for their operation: 'Well, if you gotta go, that's the way to do it.' Though *Some Like It Hot* is, from here on in, largely comedic, it continues to include dramatic moments, establishing a very specific tone that distinguishes it from many of Wilder's other farces.

In addition to its final line, punchlines are frequently threaded into the narrative, and the very first segment featuring the bootleg liquor ends with one of the best. While the above-noted revelation of the coffin's contents is done in part for its comedy, bullet holes will become increasingly significant within the film. During the raid on the Mozzarella's Funeral Parlor speakeasy at which struggling musicians Jerry and Joe are playing, they dodge a rain of bullets, but Jerry's double bass gets in the way and ends up with four bullet holes. After they witness the Saint Valentine's Day Massacre, which was perpetrated by a group of gangsters, the bullet holes become a telltale sign of the pair's identity, leaving them open to suspicion from their new bandleader Sweet Sue (Joan Shawlee) and the gangsters in the final sequence. Leading up to the film's climactic chase scene, the bullet holes foil Jerry's and Joe's disguises when gangster Spats Colombo (George Raft) discovers Jerry's double bass at the Seminole Ritz Hotel. The bullet holes represent a disturbance in the order of things, in terms of both the path of the bootleggers and the wider plot as it relates the essentialist gender divide that dictates overall society.

The scene now set – the narrative will involve Jerry and Joe on the run, a group of bootlegging gangsters out to find them, and a detective in turn on their tail – the film transforms into its promised farce. Richard Dyer writes that, like any farce, *Some Like It Hot* 'depends upon characters in the film believing in disguises that are transparent to the audience'.[1] This is very much the case, and the pair's disguises are much less thorough than, for example, Lemmon's disguise in Wilder's later film *Irma la Douce* (1963).

Wilder encouraged Curtis and Lemmon to remain unstable in their high heels, and filmed more footage than planned for their entrance to highlight their inexpertise and, according to Curtis, 'give the audience time to recover from their first laughs'.[2] This also makes it seem less likely that their disguises would be accepted, and this absurdity increases the impact of the farce.

However, even beyond the apparent comedic elements of the film, analysing Daphne (Jerry) and Josephine (Joe) must take into account that most everything, in multiple roles and fashions, is all about performance. Not only in terms of the performances of Lemmon and Curtis, which are key, but also the presence of Marilyn Monroe (playing Sugar Kane Kowalczyk), a woman whose screen and public personas were continuously and somewhat insidiously tainted by performance. Through the lens of queer theory, Some Like It Hot can be considered queer. As Alexander Doty identifies, such queer readings go beyond a narrative inclusion of cross-dressing – although, as the film's main premise, this is key – to hint at non-heteronormative desire. Doty writes that, as a genre, 'comedy is fundamentally queer since it encourages rule-breaking, risk-taking, inversions, and perversions in the face of straight patriarchal norms'.[3] Wilder and IAL Diamond's script operates in this manner, as a comedy in which characters experience and survive some extremely unlikely, even impossible, situations. As a film with a cross-dressing premise, Some Like It Hot is an extension and inversion of the classic disguise gag, which can be as simple as wearing a fake moustache.

Throughout this queer narrative and generic space, Lemmon and Curtis are actively performing layers of gender and identity, both as men and as women. Before we see their faces, Daphne and Josephine are revealed via a camera dollying behind their calves and feet, engaged in a fast pace along the glistening wet surface of a train platform. It's a framing device that is significant when considered in the context of the cinema's tendency to objectify women, because it focuses on women as a collection of body parts, rather than as whole bodies. Thus, Some Like It Hot emphasises the idea that the performance of roles is key to being accepted and understood. At the same time, in the earnestness of its farcical queerness, it suggests that you can be defined not by your outward appearance, but by accepting yourself.

In terms of these performances, Some Like It Hot has many instances that serve to alternately disrupt and advance the narrative. Heading out for a romantic evening on a private yacht in the hopes of seducing Sugar, Joe realises almost too late that in his haste to change from Josephine to Junior, the billionaire he's posing as to woo her, he has forgotten to remove his earrings. Returning from a date with millionaire Osgood Fielding III (Joe E Brown), and still in his Daphne costume, Jerry mutters to himself, 'I'm a boy … oh boy, am I a boy,' while removing his wig, so that the elements of his performance are revealed. While he probably does not actually want to wed a man, Jerry's annoyance here seems to be at the realisation that he cannot become a millionaire via marriage. Towards the end of the film, deceived by the double-bass bullet holes that reveal their identities, Jerry and Joe disguise themselves again as a bellboy and a patron of the hotel, and this time a forgotten pair of heels, worn by Jerry, gives them away.[4] In the final scene, Sugar lets Joe kiss her before she realises it's actually Josephine, and continues to knowingly kiss a woman. And famously, Osgood confirms that he still wants to be with Jerry even when he tells her he's not a woman, his response coming in the form of that celebrated final line. For Bert Cardullo, these inversions of gender and sexual attraction do not exist to suggest that homosexuality is repressed in the characters, but

It's apparent that the performance of both male and female gender roles brings the characters enjoyment, and gender distinctions begin to matter less to them as their personal relationships develop.

that adherence to patriarchal roles is quashing opportunities for fulfilment. Ergo, spurning patriarchal roles is positive, evidenced by the simple fact that being disguised as women gives Jerry and Joe the opportunity to work. Also, as Cardullo suggests, 'Daphne is Osgood's dream of the ideal woman – someone with whom he gets along so well that sex becomes beside the point.'[5] It's apparent that the performance of both male and female gender roles brings the characters enjoyment, and gender distinctions begin to matter less to them as their personal relationships develop.

And yet with Monroe as star, Some Like It Hot is very much about sex and femininity, or at least about the performance of this sexuality. Discussion of the film would not be complete without reference to the key place of Monroe in its wider narrative, as both film and star were equally important to each other. While the role came relatively late in her career, after more than a decade of supporting and lead roles, she was at the height of her fame and Sugar Kane Kowalczyk was key to Monroe's image. The character seemed to be as much the mythical Monroe as she was the fictional Sugar Kane. She plays a self-confessed 'dumb' woman and one who has allegedly been abused by the men in her life so far, which is somewhat equivalent to Monroe's own star persona. In her study of Monroe's mythological status in culture, S Paige Baty writes, 'Marilyn seems personally to have understood that her star identity was the product of invention, was in fact a dream self.'[6] Monroe in some ways performed as 'dumb' but was, as demonstrated by this self-conscious performance, quite intelligent. Her self-awareness as a female performer is very apparent in this role.

Monroe's first appearance in *Some Like It Hot* occurs at the train station, when Jerry and Joe catch a glimpse of her walking past them on their way to board a train to Miami. Here, her style and mannerisms code her both as a woman in the film desired by men, and as 'Marilyn Monroe'. To the male leads, she seems the epitome of everything they desire in a lover, and, ironically, of everything they are currently attempting to mimic while disguised as women. 'She must have some sort of built-in motor or something,' says Jerry (as Daphne), watching Sugar's hips and legs move swiftly in high heels, as the two men make observations about the demands of performing femininity. The built-in motor is, actually, a learned way of moving in line with expectations of gendered appearance, dictated by centuries of behaviour and artistic depictions; as Baty might suggest, it is a composite of elements enabled by Monroe's performance itself, and by the society perceiving Monroe and women more generally.[7] Towards the end of the film, when one of the gangsters shouts, 'Hey, that's no dame!' after realising that Joe is wearing a disguise, it not only textually acknowledges the concept of farce, but also implies that performance is inherent to gender roles and patriarchal culture. Monroe's presence, bolstered by the performances of those around her, supports these ideas.

> When one of the gangsters shouts, 'Hey, that's no dame!' after realising that Joe is wearing a disguise, it not only textually acknowledges the concept of farce, but also implies that performance is inherent to gender roles and patriarchal culture.

Identity is also performed through fashion and clothing in *Some Like It Hot*. For instance, Spats Colombo, as head of the gangsters in the film, has attained his nom de guerre via his sartorial choices. 'I sleep with my spats on,' he says, proud that his bent for sophistication means that he allegedly wears spatterdashes at all times. Other key costumes in the film were designed by Australian designer Orry-Kelly, who had already been awarded two Oscars for his work on *An American in Paris* (Vincente Minnelli, 1951) and *Les Girls* (George Cukor, 1957). Orry-Kelly had a significant and sustained career, during which he designed costumes for some of the most elegant women in Hollywood. For *Some Like It Hot*, Orry-Kelly designed Monroe's gowns, including the most iconic: a diaphanous beaded silver dress she wears during her performance of 'I Wanna Be Loved by You'. While initially unplanned, Orry-Kelly also designed Daphne's and Josephine's outfits, as per the actors' request to Wilder,[8] and he won a third Oscar, for black-and-white film costume design.

Some Like It Hot was nominated for other Academy Awards,[9] and while it failed to win more than one, it has remained an iconic and much-loved film. Wilder was a talented screenwriter, and on top of his noted debt to Lubitsch, he used certain ideas to link *Some Like It Hot* with earlier Hollywood films. When Sweet Sue complains of a stomach ulcer and tells her colleague Beinstock (Dave Barry) that the two 'new girls' – Josephine and Daphne – are 'funny', this recalls Keyes' (Edward G Robinson) suspicious ulcers in Wilder's earlier film *Double Indemnity* (1944). Towards the film's end, when the mob of gangsters sit down to dinner at their convention, Spats gestures to smash a grapefruit into a henchman's face, and here Wilder is paying homage to *The Public Enemy* (William A Wellman, 1931), one of the great early sound gangster films.[10]

While they each may settle down at the end, the two leads are on the run almost continuously, first after their workplace is raided, then from the cold weather, and later (and later again) from Spats and his cronies. Throughout, the script keeps the action flowing. In comparison to some other Wilder films that also use disguise as a key motif in the narrative, such as *The Major and the Minor* (1942), *Witness for the Prosecution* (1957) and *Irma la Douce*, the audience never has a chance to find the farce improbable in *Some Like It Hot* because it 'succeeds by virtue of its continuous motion'.[11] For instance, at the climax, Jerry and Joe change out of their menswear and into their female disguises in the seven seconds it takes to descend two floors in an elevator. On the level of an embodied, impulsive response to cinema, this comedic pacing may be a reason for the film's immediate success at the time, and its continued positive reception today. *Some Like It Hot* is Wilder's most successful, and warmest, farce. But its legacy reaches beyond the film itself, which is still remembered for its joyous and enjoyable celebration of performance, fluid identities and acceptance of self.

Eloise Ross writes and teaches in Melbourne, and holds a PhD in cinema studies from La Trobe University. She is a co-programmer of the Melbourne Cinémathèque, and editorial assistant at Screening the Past. **SE**

Endnotes

[1] Richard Dyer, *Heavenly Bodies: Film Stars and Society*, 2nd edn, Routledge, London & New York, 2004, p. 44.
[2] Tony Curtis, with Mark A Vieira, *The Making of* Some Like It Hot: *My Memories of Marilyn Monroe and the Classic American Movie*, John Wiley & Sons, Hoboken, NJ, 2009, p. 75.
[3] Alexander Doty, *Flaming Classics: Queering the Film Canon*, Routledge, New York & London, 2000, p. 81.
[4] The joke here, especially considering his first scene performing as a woman, is that Jerry is by now so comfortable wearing high-heeled shoes that he doesn't notice he is wearing them.
[5] Bert Cardullo, 'The Dream Structure of *Some Like It Hot*', *Études anglaises*, vol. 48, no. 2, 1995, p. 196.
[6] S Paige Baty, *American Monroe: The Making of a Body Politic*, University of California Press, Berkeley & LA, 1995, p. 92.
[7] ibid., p. 87.
[8] Charlotte Chandler, *Nobody's Perfect: Billy Wilder, A Personal Biography*, Applause Theatre & Cinema Books, New York, 2002, p. 210.
[9] It was nominated in the categories of Best Director (Wilder), Best Actor in a Leading Role (Lemmon), Best Writing, Screenplay Based on Material from Another Medium (Wilder and Diamond), Best Cinematography, Black-and-white (Charles Lang), and Best Art Direction, Black-and-white (Ted Haworth and Edward G Boyle).
[10] Wilder would reference this moment from *The Public Enemy* again with James Cagney's character in *One, Two, Three* (1961).
[11] Cardullo, op. cit., p. 197.

Looking for a Way Out

Reimagining the Gaze in *Carol*

GABRIELLE O'BRIEN

A look is worth a thousand words in *Carol* (Todd Haynes, 2015), in which sparse, often oblique dialogue is knowingly relegated to the periphery. Furtive glances loaded with unvoiced longing drive the narrative, and counter the oppressive male gaze associated with 1950s America and patriarchal control. The film plays on the idea of circularity, to suggest a figurative closed loop that traps women and strips them of agency. The act of looking is repeatedly mediated by windows, mirrors and other diegetic surfaces until, eventually, a female gaze emerges. This disrupts the cycle and offers the possibility of an autonomous life. The film finally breaks free of its own formal loop when Therese Belivet (Rooney Mara) and Carol Aird (Cate Blanchett) explicitly reject their socially inscribed roles, rupturing the cycle by electing to pursue a life together.

Carol is an exquisite distillation of Patricia Highsmith's 1952 novel *The Price of Salt*. Published under a pseudonym, Highsmith's treatment of a lesbian relationship dared to suggest a possible happy ending for its central characters. This boldly subverted the prevailing conservative social norms of the time; as Amber R Byers points out,

it was expected that the characters in a lesbian novel would never receive any satisfaction from a lesbian relationship. One or both usually ended up committing suicide, going insane, or leaving the relationship.[1]

Rather than replicating these narrative conventions, Highsmith filtered the criminality associated with her previous books through the lens of gender politics and sexuality. Writing at a time when same-sex relationships were considered 'obscene', the book reworked the tropes of the thriller, aligning criminal activity with the secret trysts of an illicit affair.

American auteur Todd Haynes is a highly cineliterate filmmaker who is often drawn to female characters that transgress the social mores of their time. Haynes is known for, among other things, self-reflexively using the language of melodrama as homage to Hollywood pioneers like Douglas Sirk, as evident in the referential pastiche of *Far from Heaven* (2002) and 2011 miniseries *Mildred Pierce*. Though *Carol* marks a stylistic departure for Haynes, class and identity politics remain central themes.

Haynes builds on the idea of criminality by foregrounding surveillance and watchfulness. The naturalistic aesthetic of *Carol* taps into the politics of the McCarthy era; by grounding the look of the film in period details, we are always reminded that Carol and Therese are ensnared by their surroundings. The social fabric of their world tries to pin them down with its conservative patriarchal expectations. By embedding the social 'transgression' of the women's relationship within the political landscape, Highsmith's vaguely unsettling tension is retained. The witch-hunts for communists in the US created a climate of uncertainty and paranoia; you never knew just who might be watching. *Carol*

The naturalistic aesthetic of *Carol* taps into the politics of the McCarthy era; by grounding the look of the film in period details, we are always reminded that Carol and Therese are ensnared by their surroundings.

Carol documents the relationship between young department-store shopgirl Therese and older wealthy socialite Carol. From the moment they meet, a magnetic connection develops. Carol has much to lose from pursuing Therese: her husband, Harge (Kyle Chandler), rages in frustration at her lack of interest in their marriage. Shut out of her (female-centred) world, Harge invokes a morality clause that equates Carol's sexuality with parental negligence. Their only child, Rindy (Sadie and Kennedy Heim), is used as a final gambit when Harge pushes for sole custody. With the social and emotional stakes so high, Carol's relationship with Therese takes place stealthily, furtively. As Blanchett observes, 'She has to plot each liaison as if she's plotting a crime.'[2]

plays with subjectivity and point of view to magnify the doubt associated with secretive new romantic love, and, more broadly, to echo the wariness of disclosing personal information during this era of increased surveillance.

The film opens on a note of uncertainty. The sound of a train arriving into a station signals the transition and forward momentum associated with New York City. Yet the image remains black, suggesting a tension between perception and reality. A fade-in to a close-up of an ornate pattern consolidates the idea of a misperception; the camera tilts to gradually reveal that we have been looking at a pavement grate. We are invited to reappraise the reliability of vision, as our vulnerable position is immediately made clear. This

withholding of visual information and the sense of being locked out of a complete perspective prefigures our first meeting with Carol and Therese – a scene that will be revisited at the end of the film when its significance will be made clear to the audience. In foregrounding vision, the importance of the gaze as a formal strategy in *Carol* is made explicitly clear. The relationship between bearer of the look, object of the look and mastery of the image is problematised, and by implicating the spectator in this relay, Haynes also hints at the significance of the gaze to the narrative.

The initial uncertainty surrounding the grate creates questions about its status within the streetscape. There is a tension between 'underground' repressed experience and the lively movement of the city scene above. This nods to the buried lives of marginalised communities and women generally, but alludes specifically to the emotional lives of Carol and Therese. The forward impetus of the city is aligned with the masculine world of agency and control as the camera picks out a gentleman striding across the street and tracks forward with him. There is a photo-journalistic sensibility to the muted colour palette and grainy 16mm film that channels an early 1950s visual aesthetic. This locates *Carol* within a specific time period while again emphasising the acts of looking and observation.

RESISTING THE MALE GAZE

Laura Mulvey's pioneering essay 'Visual Pleasure and Narrative Cinema' posited that Hollywood cinema panders to the gaze of heterosexual males. 'As an advanced representation system,' Mulvey wrote, 'the cinema poses questions of the ways the unconscious (formed by the dominant order) structures ways of seeing and pleasure in looking.'[3] Mulvey's psychoanalytical theory identified the male spectator (often via a male protagonist) as commander of the gaze. On screen, women are reduced to sexualised images that are then unconsciously fetishised and controlled by the male spectator.

In a world ordered by sexual imbalance, pleasure in looking has been split between active/male and passive/female. The determining male gaze projects its phantasy on to the female figure which is styled accordingly. In their traditional exhibitionist role women are simultaneously looked at and displayed, with their appearance coded for strong visual and erotic impact so that they can be said to connote to-be-looked-at-ness. *Women displayed as sexual object is the leit-motif of erotic spectacle: from pin-ups to strip-tease, from Ziegfeld to Busby Berkeley,* she holds the look, plays to and signifies male desire.[4]

The male gaze is built into the cinematic apparatus of classical Hollywood cinema, so *Carol*'s historical context chimes with Mulvey's concept. However, the film takes up a more complex temporal space – we are looking back to a past that is only imagined. The graininess of the 16mm film stock augments this fiction, bringing with it the same uncanny sensibility that comes from looking back at old photographs, accessing another time from the 'now' of the present. This dreamy quality anchors *Carol*. It is through the tangible intersection of 'then' and 'now' that resistance to the male gaze opens up and alternative subjectivities begin to filter through.

It is a male gaze that first introduces us to Carol and Therese. The camera tracks the gentleman's movement indoors to an opulent restaurant and bar. After greeting the barman with familiarity, the demarcation of male territory continues as the young man scans the space, 'hunting' with his eyes. Our point of view is collapsed with his as the camera pans left to right to replicate his vision. When he strides away to make a phone call, his dominance in the scene is heightened by his occlusion of screen space; the camera must retreat from him as he moves forward. He is signified as bearer of the look and master of the diegetic space, but this becomes problematic when he blocks our view of Carol and Therese. The mise en scène now presents the first of a repeating pattern of unwanted male attention for the pair. This intrusion is relayed to the audience as he obstructs our access to the women, blocking the wholeness of our view. In this way, Haynes puts limitations on the act of looking and disrupts our mastery of the scene. This magnifies the gentleman's misapprehension of the intimate conversation he interrupts. The male gaze that led us to Carol and Therese is compromised as the gentleman calls out to Therese. The women glance up towards the camera, their faces looking out to suggest emotional alignment. The man faces away from the camera, his head and back obstructing the foreground and unbalancing the image. The status of the women as objects (their 'to-be-looked-at-ness') is also necessarily unbalanced by his imposition in the scene.

By extension, the relationship of the audience to Carol and Therese is initially predicated on uncertainty. This disrupts the

It is here that the film formally rejects its own closed circuit, veering off course and setting off on an uncharted track. Therese goes to the party with Jack, where she is framed by windows; once again we are shut out, looking in at her but held at a distance to emphasise her sense of dislocation.

The closed loop is finally ruptured as the camera pans to follow Therese pushing past a sea of gentleman in the Oak Room. The 'hunt' of the opening sequence is now recalibrated to service a female gaze. As she searches for Carol, Therese moves with agency and momentum. She is finally steering her own course. As the point-of-view camera scans the crowd, we are anchored to Therese as our identification figure. Gone is the distance of earlier sequences; when Therese's gaze finally falls on Carol, the camera brings object, subject and audience into poignant proximity. Now the camera tracks forward through space, further collapsing our gaze with Therese's. The handheld movement conveys a frisson of excitement and fear as she approaches her lover. Her identity comes into tremulous view as she stands before Carol in an extended medium close-up. When Carol returns her look, the relationship between object and subject is dismantled, as both are cast as active lookers. The implied male spectator is shut out of this exchange by the palpable mutual desire of the two protagonists. Rather than signifying male desire, *Carol* shifts the vocabulary of the gaze to accommodate a more complicated relationship both on screen and off.

https://clickv.ie/w/screen-ed/carol

Gabrielle O'Brien is a freelance film writer and teacher. She has an MA in film studies and is a regular contributor to Screen Education. An unrepentant cinephile, she likes it best in the dark! **SE**

Endnotes

1   Amber R Byers, 'Lesbians and the 1950s', OutHistory.org, 2008, <http://outhistory.org/exhibits/show/lesbians-20th-century/1950s>, accessed 19 January 2017.
2   Cate Blanchett, quoted in Xan Brooks, 'Cate Blanchett: "I Used to Be Very Socially Awkward"', *The Guardian*, 7 November 2015, <https://www.theguardian.com/film/2015/nov/07/cate-blanchett-carol-film-interview>, accessed 3 February 2017.
3   Laura Mulvey, 'Visual Pleasure and Narrative Cinema', *Screen*, vol. 16, no. 3, Autumn 1975, p. 7.
4   ibid., p. 11, second emphasis added.
5   Phyllis Nagy, commentary, *Carol*, DVD, Universal Sony Pictures, 2016.

dwarfs the train set, suggesting her desire for control. However, this is undercut by the passing parade of female Christmas shoppers, highlighting the domestic world of women. A rapid pan allows a harried mother and child into the shot, reinforcing the patriarchal significance of mothers and daughters that *Carol* poignantly navigates.

THERESE AS 'BEARER OF THE LOOK'

We often see Carol as a fleeting reflection. Her face in close-up is mediated by external surfaces so that she becomes an image defined by her surroundings. This creates a dreamy aesthetic that again mirrors the swoony experience of first love. It also reinforces Therese's subjective viewpoint as a limiting device: she is too inexperienced to 'read' Carol as more than fantasy, echoing the trap of the male fantasy inherent in Mulvey's male gaze.

While *Carol* is not an overtly political film, its subject matter provides an inevitable commentary. For scriptwriter Phyllis Nagy, 'The chance to just engage those characters in behaviour and that behaviour becoming the political act, as it were, was very exciting to me as a dramatist.'[5] The gaze is central to Therese's journey of self-discovery; in harnessing the power of the look, she challenges the dominant order, and begins to stake out a place for herself. This is explicitly embedded in the camera lens, and by extension the cinematic apparatus, when Therese loads her camera and begins to photograph Carol. Her viewpoint is initially obstructed by the car windscreen, a nod to the voyeuristic surveillance of the period. An extreme close-up of Therese feeding film into her camera emphasises her active role, shifting the historical polarities of male/female, active/passive to reflect the women's evolving relationship. Therese literally pulls Carol into focus as she photographs her. Unlike the dreamy close-ups inside the car, Carol's entire body is now framed by Therese's camera. This suggests the emergence of a 'whole' conception of Carol – an escape from the fetishised mode of looking associated with the male gaze. The scene finishes with a subtle downward scan of Therese's eyes to take in Carol's figure. This reappropriates the objectification inherent in the male gaze, repositioning it in line with (queer) female desire.

Carol's trajectory is one of return and resistance. The film transports us back to the first scene between Carol and Therese, but we now understand the narrative chronology. A temporal conceit introduced us to the characters in the present before flashing back to chart the development of their relationship. The significance of the scene is now clear. Carol has asked Therese to come and live with her. She has separated from Harge and taken a job. She professes her love for Therese for the first time before Jack cuts in and takes control. Therese's reaction shots are this time featured, replacing the earlier sequence's measured shot / reverse shot rhythm.

Therese's gaze first lands on Carol over a toy train set in the department store where she works. Normative social expectations are embedded in the mise en scène: Therese is flanked by a wall of boxed dolls, reinforcing the binary world of gender-specific toys. An eyeline match establishes Therese's subjective point of view. Initially indistinct, Carol comes sharply into view when the camera racks focus. She suddenly intrudes on Therese's consciousness, and this action is the spark that sets Therese's own identity moving into new territory.

A medium long shot of Carol standing behind the train set emphasises the social world that will repeatedly intervene in their relationship; the shot is staged across three visual planes, allowing the bustling mass of female customers to move across the front and mid planes. In this way, Therese lacks mastery of her gaze, a reminder of the social barriers that will try to keep her and Carol apart. This is further heightened by Carol's fur jacket connoting wealth and signalling the class divide between them. Her pink scarf and hat stand out against the muted browns of the colour palette, conveying her resistance to conformity – her veiled 'Otherness'.

We often see Carol as a fleeting reflection. Her face in close-up is mediated by external surfaces so that she becomes an image defined by her surroundings.

audience is positioned to peer back at her, trying to catch a complete glimpse. We are again shut out of a cohesive viewpoint as we look in and she looks out. An eyeline match conveys Therese's point of view as she looks out at the passing cityscape. Her gaze is privileged over the limited perspective of the audience. It is Therese's subjectivity that leads the sequence, prefiguring the emergence of a discernible female gaze.

The train symbolises the 'return' ensured by a fixed circuit that is anchored in repeated movement. The image builds on the diegetic sound of the film's opening, but highlights the artificiality of escape. Its circular imagery prefigures the temporal loop that structures the film (the return to when we first meet Carol and Therese will later formally address the idea of a repeating cycle of experience). The train represents limits, but Carol's stature

controlling male gaze and replaces it with questions, prefiguring the uncertainty built into this film's form. The gentleman is identified as Jack (Trent Rowland), a friend of Therese's. He wants her to come along to a party. He stands over the women, reinforcing his position of power; however, this is subtly undercut by his position within the frame. Several looks between the women are framed by medium shots, while Jack is banished to the edge of the frame. His head remains outside of the image, emphasising the tension between social expectations and his interference in Carol and Therese's world. The women repeatedly glance at each other, but every look is circumvented by the formal composition. When Carol glances at Therese, she is captured looking towards the camera while the back of Therese's head faces the camera. This sequence is then inverted via a shot / reverse shot, which alternates back and forth between the protagonists. By not allowing us to see both women's faces simultaneously, the social barriers (class, age, sexuality) are foregrounded. This viewpoint also recalls the earlier shot taken from behind Jack's head; it visually orientates the women within their social context with its normative behavioural codes. They are trapped by the world around them.

This trap is evident in the tension between the male gaze and the female subjectivity that emerges as Therese's self-identity comes into focus. In the next scene, Therese sits in a taxi with Jack and his friends on the way to the party. Her lack of agency reduces her to an ethereal reflection, but this also protects her from the controlling male gaze that tries to pin her down. Framed by a close-up, she peers out from behind the textured surface of the rain-flecked window. The lights of the city create a superimposition that signal Therese's containment, but this in turn dilutes the mastery of the image demanded by the male gaze. The